From Sight to Sound

From Sight to Sound

Improvisational Games for Classical Musicians

Nicole M. Brockmann

Indiana University Press · Bloomington & Indianapolis

This book is a publication of

Indiana University Press
601 North Morton Street
Bloomington, IN 47404-3797 USA

http://iupress.indiana.edu

Telephone orders   800-842-6796
Fax orders   812-855-7931
Orders by e-mail   iuporder@indiana.edu

The paper used in this publication meets the
minimum requirements of American National
Standard for Information Sciences—Perma-
nence of Paper for Printed Library Materials,
ANSI Z39.48-1984.

Manufactured in the United States of America

Library of Congress Cataloging-in-Publication
Data

Brockmann, Nicole M.
    From sight to sound : improvisational
games for classical musicians / Nicole M.
Brockmann.
        p. cm.
    ISBN 978-0-253-22064-6 (pbk. : alk. paper)
1. Improvisation (Music) I. Title.
    MT68.B74   2009
    781.3′6—dc22

                                            2008035739

        1 2 3 4 5   14 13 12 11 10 09

Contents

Preface

About a decade ago, I attended a presentation on string quartet improvisation given by the Turtle Island String Quartet at the Chamber Music America conference in New York City. While I was fascinated by the techniques the group demonstrated, and I knew that the ensemble focuses heavily on jazz and other non-traditional types of quartet playing, as a primarily classical player I was also disappointed that there was little connection between the techniques that were being demonstrated and the classical repertoire that is the daily bread and butter of most string players, particularly students.

At the end of the session, when it was time for questions, I raised my hand and asked, "Are there any resources that you know of for group improvisation like this in a more traditional classical music setting?"

Blank stares were exchanged all 'round. Finally someone (I don't remember who) said, "Uh, no," and after a moment of awkward silence, they were on to the next question. To my surprise, no one in the room even seemed interested in pursuing the topic—which is, I think, indicative of the general attitude toward improvisation as it relates (or doesn't relate) to classical music.

It seemed to me that multiple-player improvisation within a common-practice harmonic setting could be a fantastic way to develop musicianship skills in ourselves and our students, if only the right logistical ground rules could be developed. For the next several years, I frittered around with various possibilities and asked my colleagues and students to try out my ideas with me.

What I didn't realize when I started the book is that while gaining the ability to improvise is valuable in itself, what's even more valuable is what improvisation teaches you about understanding music. The things you learn through developing your improvisation skills change how you think about and interact with music.

One thing I wanted to do in this book was to explicitly show how to make connections between music theory, aural skills concepts, and performance. The critical step for me, one which so often gets left out of aural skills training, is for students to realize theory and ear-training exercises on their instruments, because it is on their instruments that they are ultimately expected to express everything they are supposed to have learned in music theory and ear-training classes. Using the students' actual instruments allows them to associate a visual notation and a sonority with the kinesthetic sensation of producing that notation and sound. On a violin, for example, a minor sixth is associated with a very specific finger pattern. Constant reinforcement of the relationship between visual notation, sonority, and the kinesthetic awareness of what it would take to produce that sound on the instrument (and, by extension, a gradually developing sense of absolute pitch) leads to a multi-sensory experience and understanding of musical concepts.

Also, I wanted to stress the importance of learning to do two different things simultaneously. In the world of Dalcroze Eurhythmics, we work on this skill a lot: walking one meter while clapping another, performing rhythmic canons with ourselves, expressing different aspects of a piece with different body movements. In performance, the definitive illustration of this skill is playing and listening, which really means "playing and adjusting to what you hear." This is why many of these exercises ask students to simultaneously sing and play, or challenge them to think about what they are doing in unusual ways. They need to be able to pull back their awareness, like a camera pulling back from a movie scene, so that the technical sensations of playing are not all-consuming, but rather are understood to be part of their larger participation in a joint musical creation, one whose artistic success is as dependent on interpersonal communication and response as on the technical production of pitches.

Finally, I want to stress that this is not a book on how to improvise in the style of famous composers. Although the building blocks are the same as those used by Mozart, Mendelssohn, and Brahms, the emphasis here is not to imitate others, but to develop one's own voice. It takes practice, and patience, but the payoff is a deeper understanding of music and a confident, highly nuanced sense of musicianship that will serve you well in any professional situation.

Acknowledgments

I offer my heartfelt thanks to the following people:

To all of my teachers in the Dalcroze community, but especially Annabelle Joseph, who has been a wonderful mentor to me. I hope Marta would be proud.

To Joan Panetti, who showed me that being a musician is about far more than playing an instrument.

To my family and friends, who don't necessarily understand what the book is for but who supported me in writing it.

And most of all, to my students and colleagues over the last seven years, who cheerfully served as guinea pigs for early versions of these exercises, even if they thought I was nuts.

From Sight to Sound

1   Improvise? What For?

One of the many connections between art, music, and language is the idea of "literacy." When we describe people as "literate" in the sense of language and communication, we mean that they can both read and write. That is, they can take in information presented in written form, and they can offer back written ideas of their own, clothed in appropriate language and syntax. As musicians, we excel at the first of these two literacy skills. We read printed music and we figure out how to make our voices and instruments create aural representations of the notes on the page. Where our musical education is often sadly lopsided is in that complementary skill of creating musical ideas of our own and sharing them with others.

When we write using language, we do so for a variety of reasons. We write because our teachers have assigned us an essay or a research paper. We write in a journal to clarify our ideas or write a poem to express emotion. We write notes, letters, and e-mail to communicate with one another. Essays, research papers, poems, novels—no matter what the form, all of these involve using written language to express a concept in our own words. We choose the words that best express our ideas, figure out the right order for those words, and make sure the finished product is stylistically correct based on the rules of the genre, rules with which we are well familiar.

If we never wrote for ourselves, but only read the works of others, our understanding of language would be limited to what we could observe in those works. On the other hand, when we sit down and try to piece together a written work ourselves, we learn how diction, syntax, argument, and rhetoric work together. We learn how to develop ideas and characters, how to sustain the attention of the reader, how to create a powerful plot climax, and how to resolve loose ends in a way that leaves the reader satisfied. Writing for ourselves helps us figure out what the rules of language are and how it functions to create the effects the author intended. Our own experiences (and, sometimes, struggles) with language deepen our appreciation of masterful authors and great works of literature, which leads us to a more sophisticated understanding and enjoyment of literature as both writers and readers.

Like written literacy, true musical literacy should include both the intake and outflow of ideas using appropriate musical language and syntax. But many of us, whether professional, student, or amateur, do not feel the same sense of confident capability in response to the idea of creating our own music that we do with writing. This part of our creative musculature is generally underdeveloped. We spend days on end practicing and performing the works of others, but rarely take the initiative to play around with the building blocks of music and see what we might create with them on our own.

Yet the goals we have as creative and interpretive musicians—developing ideas over a long period, keeping the attention of the audience, delivering powerful emotional messages, and leaving the audience satisfied—are the same goals we see in good writing, and we know how much it benefits our understanding of literature to actually have hands-on experience with writing. Similarly, to achieve a more sophisticated level of musical understanding and communicative ability, we would do well to experiment with being musical creators as well as performers. Through learning to improvise our own music, with all of the bumps, bruises, awkwardnesses, and "mistakes" that come with learning any new skill, we can develop an appreciation of music that engages both intellect and emotion for ourselves and our audiences.

Just like building up injured or atrophied muscles in our physical bodies, strengthening our underdeveloped creative muscles works best when we begin slowly, developing new skills gradually and adding new challenges on top of existing strengths. No physical therapist would suggest to someone recovering from an injury that he or she should aim to climb Mt. Everest after six weeks. Similarly, beginning improvisers should not feel pressured to perform virtuosic improvisations right away, no matter how accomplished they are in other technical aspects of performance.

Contrary to popular myth, improvisation has almost nothing to do with virtuosic playing, and everything to do with virtuosic listening. Since it is based on hearing, a skill that every musician must possess, anyone can learn to do it, regardless of whether you have been playing an instrument for four years or forty. The relationship between improvisation and listening is simple: if you can hear and understand what is going on around you, you can jump into the sandbox and play with others. This requires neither perfect pitch nor virtuosic fingers. No matter what your level, learning improvisation and the skills that come with it will hone your musicianship as well as your technique.

This approach to improvisation emphasizes the value of the process, not the result. The goal of doing the exercises and games in this book is not to execute the most perfect brand-new composition ever conceived. Instead, you will discover the sheer fun of creating your own music, realize and experience the inner workings of how musical elements go together, and develop confidence in your own abilities to hear and respond.

Too many musicians dismiss this experience out of hand, sure that classical improvisation is impossibly complicated, that they wouldn't know where or how to begin, and that they wouldn't be able to produce anything good. They are so bogged down by inhibitions, timidity, awkwardness, fear of failure, or doubt in their own creative abilities that they have lost their sense of their own creative potential. This is sometimes an unfortunate side effect of years of rigid and regimented training, in which students spend endless hours drilling repetitive passages and learning how to conform to the expectations of teachers and audition committees.

Improvisation can have a profound effect on these frustrated and discouraged musicians when they discover how easy it is to do and do successfully. Improvisation actually starts being fun. As your skills grow, you become more confident in your ability to hear and respond, and doubts and inhibitions start to seem less important. You will feel the freedom to experiment and the confidence to take risks without fear of making a mistake. Not only is there no shame in making mistakes while learning to improvise, but mistakes are actually essential; they show us how we might want to correct course. It's not always easy to determine whether a sound was what you wanted, but it's usually quite clear when it was *not* what you wanted! In improvisation there is always a way to turn an unintended note into a window of opportunity onto something new and interesting, so you don't have to think of those notes as "mistakes" at all.

When performers begin to see improvisation as an ongoing study in musicianship rather than a brilliant display of technique, they forget many of their fears, particularly the fear of not being able to create "perfect," virtuosic improvisations. Creating your own music through improvisation is just another way of expressing the same elements of musicianship that you use every day in interpreting pieces written by others. By themselves, our instruments and voices only create sound, not music. The things that turn the sounds into music—phrasing, direction, tone color, rhythmic vitality—come from you, whether you are improvising your own melody or playing a Prokofiev sonata or a Mozart quartet. The nuances you infuse into your playing, those elements that make your performance different from anyone else's and that form your musical personality, are the raw elements of the musical voice that will emerge when you improvise.

Traditions of Improvisation in Classical and Jazz Music

Another objection many classical musicians raise regarding improvisation is that as a performance technique, improvisation seems to belong firmly to the realm of jazz. Yet it is only within the last century or two that improvisation has faded from the classical arena due to changing trends in composition and performance practice. There is much rich scholarship on this topic, but the following very brief synopsis of overall trends in Western art music will serve as a basic primer.

Improvisation has been a part of Western music since the beginning of written music in the medieval period. It grew in popularity during the Renaissance, when it became a core feature of both secular and sacred music in various vocal and instrumental combinations. As the Renaissance gave way to the Baroque, improvisation became particularly important in instrumental music as a means of creating variations on a theme, a compositional technique used heavily in the creation of chaconnes and passacaglias. Improvisation was also required for the realization of the figured bass notation of Baroque keyboard continuo parts. During the Baroque and Classical eras, improvisation in the context of actual concert performance became a combination of art form and parlor trick; celebrated composers demonstrated their intellectual and technical facility by improvising complex polyphonic forms such as toccatas and fugues at the keyboard. Bach, Handel, Mozart, and Beethoven were all well known for their improvisational abilities, and the tales told about these and other composers' legendary improvisational abilities have certainly helped foster our modern-day anxiety about the subject. During the Classical era, when the instrumental concerto began to flourish, important thematic material of works was used as the basis for performers' improvisations of elaborate cadenzas for the solo instrument.

During the nineteenth century, instrumental improvisation began to decline as a result of the changing relationship between composers and performers. In earlier musical traditions, composers and performers had shared the responsibility for interpretation of a piece. Composers sketched out the big ideas, and performers took pride in the skill of their improvisations over that skeletal outline. As the Classical era gave way to the Romantic, successive generations of composers sought more and more control over exactly how their music was to be played. They specified every note and ornament, and wrote out their own cadenzas in exacting detail. The development of forms such as the fantasia and the impromptu showed the paradoxical desire of composers both to control every aspect of a performance and to create the impression of improvisatory freedom. Some composers, including Mendelssohn and Liszt, continued to improvise in their own styles, but improvisation on the part of performers had virtually disappeared from the scene by the end of the nineteenth century.

Improvisation found a new home with the birth of jazz, where it became a powerful expression of freedom and individual identity as well as technical skill. The technique and genre are so deeply intertwined that many modern classical musicians associate improvisation exclusively with jazz, forgetting that this is a musical heritage which they originally shared as well. Compositional trends in art music within the last century show renewed interest in improvisation, though many of these explorations have gone beyond the bounds of the tonal improvisation explored in this work.

This book focuses on techniques for improvisation using the structures of common-practice harmony. In order for the study and art of improvisation to be as meaningful as possible to the classical artist, it must relate to the style of music that is the practicing musician's normal milieu. Learning the rich tradition of jazz improvisation is certainly rewarding, but most classical musicians do not play jazz as part of their meat-and-potatoes study. And although there is a growing circle of chamber music groups specializing in contemporary music, most performers and ensembles still rely on the works of the eighteenth, nineteenth, and early twentieth centuries for their core repertoire. Improvising within the setting of common-practice harmony and style brings to life the musical issues that most classical musicians deal with every day, and the lessons learned about phrasing, pacing, direction, melody, and harmony can be applied to music of any era.

We cannot leave this portion of our discussion without recognizing one group of classically trained musicians that has successfully maintained an ongoing tradition of improvisation: organists. The persistence of improvisation in organ music is largely due to the tremendous role church music has played in the daily life and training of organists. The organ has been the keyboard instrument of choice in church music for hundreds of years, and it is a rare organist whose resume does not include some experience in this genre. Flexibility is a key element in church music, since one of its roles is to support elements of the ceremony. The organist must be able to tailor the music to the rite through improvisation. As long as there is a need for a musical tradition, that tradition will continue; improvisation in church music has survived because it is still needed for both musical and practical reasons.

Getting Started with Improvisation

Because improvisation has been so much less prominent in classical music in the last few centuries, it is no longer a common skill that all performers are expected to master. As long as we see improvisation as a virtuosic technical challenge, it can fill even some of the most accomplished performers with needless dread and anxiety. If your vision of improvisation is standing alone on a concert stage under a glaring spotlight wearing a deer-in-the-headlights expression, of course you will feel awkward and nervous. No one wants to perform under those circumstances. But if we change how we think about improvisation, and the environment in which we practice and learn it, we can transform it from an anxiety-inducing event into something fun and spontaneous.

The ideal environment for improvisation is one that is familiar and supportive, in which each musician feels comfortable taking risks and trying new ideas. One reason that these exercises are written for multiple players working together is that the social dynamics of the small ensemble or chamber music setting are familiar and comfortable enough to most musicians that no one is likely to feel he or she is on the hot seat. And since all parts are improvised simultaneously, all players are in the same boat of having to create their own parts. This setting is also ideal because chamber music is one of the most social forms of music-making. Departing from the isolation of solo playing or the cattle-call dynamics sometimes found in the orchestral world, chamber music is an environment that requires balancing individual performances within the context of ensemble playing. The chamber music setting is the perfect laboratory in which to practice and understand how improvisation can improve your ears, your technique, and your musicianship.

When working with this book, remember that these exercises are not "one-shot deals." Each game is meant to be played numerous times so that you can decide what you liked, what you didn't like, and what you want to try again the next time. When you are starting out, think of improvisation as educated guessing. When you are making up a melody, you do need to have a general idea of where it's going. You need to know your harmonic destination and have an idea of the journey you will need to take to get there. Since this kind of knowledge and familiarity comes about through repetition, you may need to play each exercise through several times in order to get the harmonies in your ear. If you're unsatisfied with your improvisation, or you can think of a way to make it better, do it again—and again, and again.

The best way to start improvising is with a lot of structure and a little freedom, so that you don't feel overwhelmed. The beginning games are simple, without virtuosic technical demands. They are designed to wake up your ear and encourage active hearing. The exercises progress to improvisations based on familiar building blocks, such as scales and arpeggios. These should help increase your confidence so that your comfort level with hearing, playing, and singing is much higher by the time you are ready for improvisations with your group as a whole. As you progress, you will need less and less structure. You will also come to rely more on your ears and less on your eyes to tell you if your improvisation fits within a harmonic progression.

These games are intended to be challenging enough to keep your interest and concentration at a high level, but not so difficult that they cause only frustration. They follow the formula that a lot of comfort and a little bit of challenge produces growth. Each time you successfully perform a task at a level slightly above your comfort threshold, you will gain confidence and your limits will be pushed back a little further. Tasks that at first seemed impossible will become manageable and even easy. In each game, the basic rules are explained first, with variations presented at the end to increase the challenge. The exercises should never become routine or humdrum, so as soon as you have mastered the basic rules, use the variations to stimulate your creative abilities in a slightly different way. Some of the variations are complex enough to completely change the dynamics of the game. Above all, remember that they are called "games" because they're meant to be fun!

Improvisation and Chamber Music

This book was written with the chamber music setting in mind because chamber music exemplifies the perfect balance of solo and ensemble skills. In solo playing, you control every aspect of the performance. You control the shape of the line, the proportion of the ritards, and the timing of the phrases. Even when you are playing a concerto with orchestra, your solo line reigns supreme. Convention dictates that the orchestra adjust to your tempo and your rubato. As a member of an orchestra, on the other hand, you see the other extreme: almost all musical decisions are made by the conductor, and your job is to execute what he or she has decided. There is little opportunity for you to place your personal musical stamp on any performance, particularly if you are a string player buried in the middle of the section.

These two dynamics are balanced in chamber music, in which an ensemble texture is produced from the interweaving of individual lines. While you do not have the autocracy of the soloist, neither can you sit back and rely on someone else to make all the musical decisions. Each line, whether melody, bass, or harmony, contributes to the shaping of the overall work. This is why you must be an active participant in all aspects of the music. Even if the melody is not yours to play, your intentional involvement is critical to the success of the work.

When we are unsatisfied with our performance of a particular phrase or section, it often indicates that we have not yet discovered which questions to ask about the goal or effect of the phrase. We may be reading the words of a sentence, but not really understanding its meaning; it therefore becomes very difficult to adequately communicate that meaning to a listener. Start by asking yourself what you find "wrong" with your performance of that phrase. What is strange or uncomfortable? What are you dissatisfied with? Is it a phrasing issue? Direction? Sound quality? Flow? Then look at the score to see if you can find what's going on compositionally that makes this particular part not what you expected. Why do you think the composer made that choice? Did he or she want the listener to feel uncomfortable there? Sometimes, the answer is yes. In this case, you might want to think of ways that you could vary your tone, pacing, dynamics, or other nuances to try to intensify the effect. On the other hand, if you think the composer's intent was not to make the listener uncomfortable, then you will have to search out ways to adjust the energy and direction of the phrase so that the listener is left feeling satisfied.

Through your explorations of these issues, you will begin to make correlations between your instinctive musical feelings and your intellectual reasoning. The most effective musical decisions are those in which the heart and brain cooperate. Conventional wisdom dictates that a performance that is all head and no heart will not likely be satisfying to most audiences. What fewer musicians recognize is that the reverse is also true: exclusive reliance on instinct, without intellectual support, leads to musical choices that lack the integrity to stand on their own. Performances in this vein are sometimes unflatteringly described as random, capricious, and maudlin, and the performer can offer no greater justification for his or her decisions than "I just felt it that way, but I can't explain it." Should another player in the group "just feel" the phrase differently, a stalemate occurs, as neither player has any rational means of convincing the other of the validity of his or her interpretation. If instinct is used as the ultimate determinant of musicality, without the support of intellectual understanding, then there is no method by which compromises can be reached or alternatives considered. Both intellectual discernment and intuitive response are necessary for true musicianship.

Another advantage to improvising within a small-group setting is that it gives many musicians the chance to do what they could not do alone: improvise within a harmonic framework. Hands-on experimentation with harmony is extremely valuable, and musicians who play single-line instruments often miss out on this experience simply because the logistics of their instrument makes it impossible for them to produce two independent musical lines. There is also a marvelously playful element of surprise in group improvisations: when you are improvising with others, you are never completely in control. This give-and-take of stimulus and response is an essential element of improvisation, and the sudden bursts of laughter that so often happen in the middle of a game add immeasurably to the fun of the whole experience.

Applications and Relevance

Improvisation is relevant for the practicing musician on several different levels. It will banish your inhibitions and free your creative powers. It will help you better understand how music is constructed, from both intellectual and aural perspectives. It will develop your sense of line and phrasing. It will sharpen your ear and help you gain technical facility on your instrument. It may save you in a performance situation, in case of a memory slip or a fumbled page turn. And because improvisation training will give you a heightened sense of control over the music you make, it might even help reduce performance anxiety.

Improvising within a certain style also helps you truly assimilate that style. Looking at a piece of music in an unfamiliar style is like reading a set of driving directions to a place you're visiting for the first time. The directions tell you to turn left at the third light, drive two miles, go around the traffic circle, etc. Since you don't know the neighborhood, you are completely dependent on the directions to get you where you want to go, and, since you have never seen your destination, you may not even know if you have gotten there! Improvisation, on the other hand, is like exploring the neighborhood and learning the landmarks. You learn that in the Classical neighborhood the streets are generally laid out in a regular grid, whereas a few miles away in the Romantic neighborhood, they curve in unexpected directions. You will also learn that the traffic laws are quite different in each neighborhood, and that you will have to change your driving style accordingly. (Over there in the Contemporary neighborhood, for example, some places seem to have suspended traffic rules altogether.) Improvisation will take you to your destination, but it will also show you alternative routes and alternative destinations. By familiarizing yourself with the environment using improvisation, you develop the ability to intuitively navigate through the musical neighborhood.

Improvisation can also be used as a step in the process by which you learn a piece of music. It can help you make musical decisions about a piece you are working on alone or with your ensemble. You may occasionally come across a phrase that stubbornly refuses to lie right, or a transition you can't seem to manage properly. Isolating the troublesome bars and improvising on them can help for a number of reasons. When you put a new melody to an existing harmonic progression, you will hear the progression in a new light. This will bring out harmonic aspects of the phrase that you hadn't heard before because you were too busy concentrating on the difficulties of your part. It will also isolate the composed melody and allow you to study its features in comparison to your improvised one. Both the similarities and the differences between the two lines will help you identify the salient qualities of the composed phrase. For example, your line and the composer's might be built on the same scale fragment, but the composer might have thrown in a curve ball by displacing one or more notes into a lower octave. When you compare multiple versions of a melodic line, those small details stand out in sharp relief and beg to be examined more closely. Once you begin to appreciate the musical nuances of the composed melody, you will be able to choose and implement the technical adjustments needed to express them.

This approach works with harmony as well as with melody. You can zero in on the colors of particular harmonies in a phrase by replacing them with other harmonies and improvising on the new progression. This is an excellent way to really hear the effects of different predominants. The same progression will take on an entirely different color when you replace a IV chord with a ii, a V/V, or an augmented sixth chord. This in turn should prompt a different quality of expression for each color. It will also help you discern the phrase structure; ask yourselves, "What if Beethoven had used an authentic cadence here instead of a deceptive one? What would that have done to the flow of the music, and how would it have affected the way we play that phrase?" Hearing the different effect of your improvisation helps you understand and appreciate the particulars of the original.

Classical improvisation can even have a place in the concert hall. Some of the more advanced games for ensembles as a whole make engaging impromptu encores after a concert performance, and even allow the audience to get involved.

Improvisation and Musicianship Training

Although you can certainly become a competent player without learning improvisation, this kind of training will develop the skills that separate a player who is outstanding from one who is merely good. Some musicians argue that there is no real need for improvisation training in the world of today's working classical musician, since most players are not called upon to improvise in a performance setting as part of their daily routine. Then again, most musicians don't have to sight-sing every day, but it is still required in most colleges and conservatories because we know that the learning process involved in this study makes our students better musicians. The emphasis on improvisation and composition as part of the 2003–2004 National Association of Schools of Music standards for instruction for students in all professional undergraduate music degree programs shows that accrediting agencies are beginning to consider this kind of training to be an essential part of a complete education in music.

Most music programs at the college or conservatory level approach education through two main questions: "why" and "how." Academic courses tend to address the question of "why": Why do certain sonorities go together to create a phrase? Why does one chord create a feeling of tension and another a feeling of resolution? Why do phrases behave as they do? The other side of the coin, the "how" of music, is generally the province of the studio teacher, who helps students find the technical means of expressing their musical ideas. This is not to say, of course, that the studio teacher is only a technician. Frequently the studio teacher is the student's most direct source of musical inspiration. Nevertheless, it is usually in the weekly lesson, not the solfège classroom, that the student learns the physical ways to use bow, breath, or touch to capture the essence of a phrase.

Although it is convenient to separate studio classes from academic work in terms of the classroom dynamics and skills needed for each, there is no real dividing line between the questions of "why" and "how." The border between them is often so blurry that each area spills over into the other. A question raised in one realm may even have its answer in another. Say that John, a string student, is having trouble figuring out what to do with the bow in order to shape a phrase properly. He thinks he is doing everything right, but his ears tell him that his performance of the phrase is not convincing. The answer may lie in examining the phrase from a compositional standpoint, since there are other things going on in the music that influence how the solo line should be played. In the case of our imaginary piece, John may realize upon studying the score that the composer has written a nine-bar phrase instead of the eight-bar one John expected, with a harmonic rhythm that prolongs certain harmonies in ways that John was not accommodating in his phrasing. The stretching out of the phrase over one extra bar will compel John to adjust how he manages the bow and how he applies weight and speed to it in order to draw out the arc of the phrase over one more measure. Very often, "how" questions have "why" answers; we may notice a problem from a technical standpoint, but solving it requires understanding the musical structure so that we can choose what kind of technical adjustments to make.

Because of the overlap of "why" and "how," academic and studio teachers often share the teaching of musicianship concepts like phrasing, direction, tension and resolution, and rubato. The difference between the two approaches is that each addresses musical issues from a different point along the continuum of musical activity. This continuum runs from composition at one end to performance at the other. Energy can flow both ways on the activity spectrum, from composition to performance and back again, with each informing the other. (This is particularly evident if you are lucky enough to be able to work with a composer.)

There is also a temporal aspect to this continuum. Unlike the quality of musical energy, which can flow either way, temporal energy only flows in one direction: from composition (the musical act which takes place at the earliest point on our timeline) to the performance of the composed work, which may occur anywhere from days to years later. Academic courses tend to explore musical questions from a vantage point near the composition end of the continuum, studying the actual building blocks of pieces as written with an eye toward their future performance. Studio teaching, on the other hand, inhabits the other end of the continuum, addressing issues of performance with the understanding of compositional issues as a backdrop.

Improvisation is a unique way to develop musicianship skills because it allows us to experience the "why" and the "how" simultaneously. It negates the delay between music's composition and its performance, since in improvisation, the moments of composition and performance are one and the same. Improvisation is conception and realization happening simultaneously.

The Role of Roman Numeral Analysis

One of the goals of this book is that you gain a heightened awareness of structural harmony through learning to recognize chordal sonorities and progressions both by eye and by ear. Many of these exercises ask you to do a Roman numeral analysis of the progressions used in the game. Like improvisation itself, harmonic analysis is a topic that makes some people cringe. They remember dull theory classes, innumerable voice-leading rules, and the headaches of deciphering figured-bass notation. Every year, with the turning of the leaves in September, a plaintive cry rises up from first-year music theory and aural skills classrooms in colleges and music conservatories across the country: "I don't understand why I have to learn this."

To many of these students, whose love of performing music inspired them to pursue it as a career, music theory and aural skills seem but dull drudgery, stifling their creativity by wrapping it up in rules, regulations, and red pen. Students often really don't understand why they have to learn harmonic analysis, because they don't see how the music they love is connected to Roman numerals and symbols. So they plug away resentfully at their harmonization exercises, semester after semester, year after year. At the end of their coursework, if they have applied themselves diligently, they may be able to look at a piece of music and announce definitively that the harmony in bar seven is a ii half-diminished six-five chord. For many, this represents the long-awaited end of their studies in analysis. The theory book goes back on the shelf, to gather dust and eventually be donated, yellowed with age and disuse, to a neighbor's yard sale. But there are other students, looking at the same ii half-diminished six-five chord, who see another question rather than an answer: "So what?"

Although it seems flippant, "so what?" is one of the most astute questions of true musical analysis, because it reflects the fact that the ultimate goal of all musical activity is performance. After all, most composers write music to be played, not because it looks pretty on the page. The supreme realization of any harmonic analysis is its actual performance. The musically curious performer looks at a score and says, "Yes, that's a ii half-diminished six-five chord, but so what? What does that mean to my performance? Why did the composer choose that particular harmony? What effect is produced by that sonority, and what should I do technically to express that effect? How does my melody flow through that harmony, and how does the harmony color my line?"

From a musicianship standpoint, the purpose of analysis is to identify exactly what's going on in the music, transforming a succession of sonorities in time into a linear chain of symbols on a page. A good analysis is almost an art form in itself—a visual representation of the defining colors and patterns of the music and a snapshot of its structure.

Individual Roman numerals are like words in a language. Each symbol represents a particular sonority and function, like different parts of speech. A V chord relates to a I chord like a preposition to its object. And, as in language, the meaning of the individual symbols is transformed when they are combined to create a sentence that expresses a central idea. The communicative possibilities of a complete phrase depend on the particular combination of its component sonorities, illustrating the principle that the whole is much greater than the sum of its parts.

Roman numerals communicate information on a variety of levels. We normally think of them as a means of providing vertical information about a certain chord: its root, its modality or quality, its inversion, and whether there are any chromatic or added pitches. But they also provide vital information about the horizontal aspect of music: how the sonorities relate to each other as they progress through time. One of the most important attributes of Roman numerals is their ability to indicate relative harmony. This is crucial because Western harmony is a relative science: we understand harmonic progressions based on how chords relate to other chords, not by the sound of each chord standing alone. No matter what the absolute pitches are in certain chords, they can share the same relative function. A dominant seventh chord in the key of C has the same sonority as a dominant seventh chord in the key of A, though the pitches are different. For this reason, Roman numeral analysis of a chord is always dependent on function.

Unfortunately, determining the function of a sonority is not always easy. Though there are many advantages to the Roman numeral system, it lacks the vocabulary to express every musical idea, and trying to make every element in a phrase conform to Roman numeral analysis can sometimes be cumbersome or inappropriate. Assigning a Roman numeral to a chord implies that it has a certain structural importance in the phrase, when this is not always true. Sometimes chords are formed by the casual meeting of two or more horizontal lines; there may be a whole series of chords born in this manner that are merely pleasing scenery on the way from one structural sonority to another. In these instances, Roman numerals might be reserved for key places of harmonic importance: places of arrival or places in which the phrase turns a certain direction or where a particular color is introduced. The pivotal harmonies of each phrase combine to create a road map of the entire piece.

There are also musical moments that "work" aurally but not necessarily functionally, often based on kinds of resolution and tension that don't always fall into Roman numeral categories. The ear and the brain understand the relationships between sonorities, even if the fingers cannot notate them neatly. Music written outside the common-practice period is full of non-traditional and unorthodox groupings of harmonies. As with all other aspects of musicianship, let your ears and your common sense be your guide.

The most compelling argument for understanding Roman numeral notation will come when you first experience the connection between symbol and meaning. There is an anecdote which relates the moment in which the young Helen Keller, blind, deaf, and mute, first understood that when her teacher tapped on her palm, she was trying to communicate with her. This realization took place when her teacher repeatedly tapped the signal for "water" on Helen's hand and then thrust it into the cold spout of water from a pump. In that instant, Helen understood that her teacher's taps on her palm weren't just patterns of sensation, but that they meant something tangible and real. This was the moment in which Helen's world opened wide. You can reach this "aha!" moment with harmonic notation when you begin to make connections between the visual symbol and the sound. Once you have done this, you will understand music at a different level, because you will begin to have a sense of its underlying structure.

Learning to recognize patterns of sonorities by ear is probably one of the most challenging aspects of musicianship training, but it is also one of the most important. Too often students will be able to recognize a chord on the page, but cannot pick it out from a series of other chords played at the piano. How much more powerful your ear becomes when the information it receives does not have to be filtered through your eyes before it is understood by your brain!

Preliminary Exercise: On Leading and Following (a game for 2 or more people)

Leading and following skills are very important in chamber music playing, but targeting and training these skills is sometimes difficult. After starting a new kind of physical activity, many of us have probably said, "I hurt muscles I didn't even know I had!" Our leading and following skills are much like these muscles: we don't think about them most of the time, but at critical moments their weakness is revealed.

The following exercise will wake up your ears and isolate leading and following abilities. It is presented as an example before any of the ear-training or improvisational games because the success of each subsequent game depends on your ability to both lead and follow. The key to mastering both skills is the same: active listening and awareness of an organic pulse.

Choose a piece that you are currently working on, one that you know fairly well. It might be a sonata or concerto movement, or a string quartet or other ensemble piece. Select an excerpt about 24–32 bars in length. Play through the excerpt once as you normally do.

Then, select one person to be the leader. On your next play-through, the leader will be responsible for making the tempo faster or slower at will. The others must stay glued to the leader. You will each have a turn at being leader and follower, so read the information on both roles carefully. Let's start our investigation by looking at the classic melody/accompaniment scenario, in which the person with the melody at any given moment is generally the leader and those with the accompaniment are generally followers.

FOLLOWERS An important element of following is anticipation: knowing what's in the leader's part, knowing how your part fits with his or hers, and, most importantly, adjusting to fit what he or she has done. Even among professional musicians, there are many who have never bothered to learn this skill.

A great melody is not just a collection of pitches and rhythms. It has a shape, an energy, and a direction. A computer can reproduce the pitches and rhythms of a Schubert art song or a Beethoven sonata, but what makes that collection of pitch and rhythmic data turn into music is the shape, energy, and direction that a human performer puts into it. The computer can play the notes and rhythms, which are fixed quantities. But a human being can add the extra dimension of changing and adjusting the direction of the melody in time, which is necessary because truly expressive melodies are rarely absolutely metronomic. Some notes rush ahead, while others linger and hold back. These distortions of absolute tempo last only tiny fractions of seconds, so mastering the subtlety of minute rubato is musicianship at the highest level.

This is as true for accompanimental voices as it is for melodies. The rhythms and harmonies of the inner voices must shape themselves to the melody. Some musicians sit dutifully counting rests, waiting until their entrance with ears and brain turned off, and come in when their counting (not their ears) tells them it's time. In doing so, these players sometimes crash into the melody, which may have required a tiny extra moment for a harmony to bloom or a phrase to settle. This is jarring to the audience and annoying to fellow musicians, because it indicates that those players were not really listening.

Sensitivity to rubato does not mean, of course, that you should throw your sense of pulse away. The coherence of the work as a whole depends on the ordered presentation of musical ideas in time. But music is rarely static. Like a leaf caught in a stream, it rushes forward when the energy of the current is strong and clear, slows when there is a bend in the flow of the water, and hangs suspended for a timeless instant over a waterfall. Imposing rigid counting on an essentially fluid phrase does not often yield good results. When you go with the line, your accompaniment part takes on the color and motion of the melody. In this symbiotic relationship, each gives the other life. This makes the accompaniment as interesting as the melody, and sometimes even more interesting.

The practical implication of this for those who are "followers" in this setting is that you need to adjust your pulse, sound, energy, and sense of pacing to those of the person who is leading, generally the melody player. In chamber music, the exact placement and degree of rigidity of the pulse is always a group decision. Each player must combine a strong internal sense of pulse with the flexibility to bend to others. Try to figure out what the melody player will need the accompaniment to do in order to be as expressive as possible. How do the notes of the melody fit together? Where do you sense the melody wants to pull back or run forward, and how can you offer your playing to support the effect? It is not a question of giving up your independence or becoming a blind slave to someone else's musical desires. If you hear the flow of the line in a different way, suggest it! If you hear something special in your line that you'd like to bring out, do it! If that means you need a little extra time or a change in balance or texture, ask for it! The goal is to arrive at a musical conception that everyone can agree is satisfying, and the only way to reach that goal is for each person to share his or her ideas. Music-making is a collaborative experience.

LEADER   Many people make the error of taking a dictatorial approach to leadership, both musically and personally. Don't get your ego wrapped up in the act of leadership or think that the job of the leader is to tell others what to do. All players are after the same collaborative end: working jointly to create a beautiful musical experience in which each player feels satisfaction and ownership. In the business world, good leaders are those who are able to help their employees and colleagues succeed. The musical version of this is not so far removed: good leaders are ones who play beautifully and who enable their colleagues to play beautifully as well. Your colleagues will not be able to play beautifully if they can't find or follow you, or if they don't feel that their contributions are valued.

In this preliminary game, the variable is tempo. You will be able to move ahead or pull back, and the rest of the ensemble will learn how to respond and adjust to you. Manipulating tempo is like reeling in a struggling fish on a line: it must be done gradually or something will break. Tempo has inertia, and if you try to move it too much too soon, the ensemble will unravel. The disorientation and queasiness that come from going from 0 to 60 mph in a few seconds are a fine thrill—if you're on a roller coaster, not in a rehearsal hall. When you lead, remember that others are relying on you and watching closely to see what you will do. They must be able to sense your pulse; otherwise, they will be helpless to support you, which is frustrating both for you and for them. Always show your pulse, both physically (through body language, cueing, and eye contact) and musically (through direction and quality of sound).

This seems like commonsense advice that shouldn't need to be taught, but it is surprising how many real-world performers absolutely trample their colleagues in rehearsal and performance. Once, when I didn't have directions to a concert venue, I asked to follow another musician ("Robin") in my car. We had played together many times, and although I liked Robin, I was constantly frustrated by her tendency to rush forward with the melody without regard for what the other musicians were doing and without including them in the decision-making process. This tendency held true for driving as well; Robin's car had peeled out of the parking lot before I even had my key in the ignition. I was completely lost. In a prime example of life imitating art, Robin had just taken off without giving me the slightest chance to follow.

When whoever is playing the melody behaves as Robin did, it makes the other musicians feel frustrated and angry. Most chamber music players want to play together. They love the experience of playing in tandem with another person and are happy to follow someone's lead if it is clearly communicated. Let your colleagues know what's coming so they can adjust to you. If you make it impossible for others to play with you, then you are not really playing chamber music.

Now play through the excerpt you have chosen, with the leader moving ahead or pulling back and the others following. You will probably see that there are limits to how quickly and severely you can change the tempo and not lose one another. As your ensemble improves, try to increase the variability of tempo without losing cohesion. Tempo is only one quality that can be varied in this way; when you are experts in manipulating tempo, add other elements, such as dynamics and sound quality. Or, memorize the excerpt and try playing it with your eyes closed. This variation forces you to rely on your listening skills alone.

Keep these elements of good chamber music musicianship in mind as you play through the exercises and games in this book. By the end of the book, not only will you have learned to improvise, you will have learned how to be a true chamber musician.

About the Games in This Book

The games in this book are designed to give you an idea of the many different ways in which improvisation can help develop your musicianship. Once you have mastered the games as they are presented, develop your own variations to push your limits even further. Some exercises include suggested variations, but you need not limit yourself to these. When you have mastered improvisations on chord progressions presented in the major mode, try them in the minor mode, and see how the flavor of the progression changes. You are encouraged to find as many alternative solutions to each challenge as you can. Each variation is a lesson in itself.

The exercises are divided into four main categories: Building Listening Skills; Simple Melodic Improvisations; Melody and Harmony: Improvisations for Ensembles; and From Sight to Sound: Getting off the Page. The games appear in generally progressive order, with the easier ones at the beginning of each section and the more difficult ones toward the end. Because everyone has different abilities, you may not all agree on which games are the hardest. You will quickly find out which challenges you can meet easily and which ones are likely to give you trouble. It is not necessary to stick to an absolutely linear progression through the book; you may benefit from jumping forward and backward as needed.

Although the language used here is mostly that of instrumental performance rather than vocal, almost every game in this book is perfectly well suited for singers, or for singers and instrumentalists working together. Singers should feel free to substitute the word "sing" for "play" when working with the exercises. Vocalists may use either fixed- or movable-do solfège, or may sing without syllables if desired. Most of the ensemble games were written using the string quartet as a model, but they are adaptable to many other combinations of instruments. A few of the exercises are specific to certain instruments because of the technical demands required, but the piano may always be used. Games marked for four or more players could also be done with fewer, particularly if piano is involved. Feel free to alter the instructions as needed to conform to the demands of your particular ensemble.

Using a variety of tempi and textures will vary the feel of your improvisations. Slow and fast improvisations each present their own challenges. By exploring different dynamics, pitch registers, meters, colors, and styles of articulation, you ensure that your improvisations will never be dull, and that no two will sound alike.

Improvisations are always to be executed musically: that is, with phrasing, dynamics, rubato, direction, and all the other nuances that are part of good musicianship. This requires a high level of attention on the part of all players. When rehearsing composed music, players become familiar with the curve of the melody and the pacing of the accompaniment through practice and repetition. In improvisation, however, exact repetition will rarely occur, so try to pick up as many aural and body language cues as you can the first time around. Sharpen your ears and your instincts and play your part as if you were in someone else's shoes. Anticipate what their musical choices might be, but don't impede them if they surprise you with a different decision.

In order to avoid the book getting too bogged down with instructions, some of the details of gameplay have been left for you to discover. Your musicality and common sense will help you decide how certain logistical niceties should be handled. Make your own decisions and find ways that work for your group. Any solution that works is a good solution.

A note on "perfect" or "absolute" pitch: Although players with perfect pitch are sometimes thought to have an advantage in the musical world, relative pitch is just as valuable here. Some people with absolute pitch never learn to develop their sense of relative pitch, and they miss out on an important aspect of music: the relationships between notes. If you have perfect pitch, you will find some of the introductory exercises easier, but you may have more difficulty with games that rely on relative pitch. Games requiring transposition may be particularly challenging. Developing your relative pitch will help you understand how chords work together by enabling you to sense the relative movement of different lines. This is a horizontal method of analysis rather than a vertical one, and is based on the relationship of pitches to each other rather than to their place in a fixed system.

That being said, however, absolute pitch is often a useful tool, and you may wish to work toward developing it. The more you develop your ear, the more you will learn to recognize absolute pitches. Try this experiment: Every day for a month, once or twice a day, try to sing an A out of the blue. Remember the last time you heard it—maybe it was the oboe player tuning the orchestra, or the opening notes of Mendelssohn's "Italian" Symphony, or the first note of Paganini's 24th Caprice. In addition to the actual pitch, try to recall the quality of the sound; if it was produced by an oboe it will have a very different timbre than if it was produced by a piano or a violin. The more sensory details you bring to your recollection, the more accurate it will be. Can you remember who was playing the oboe in your memory? What did he or she look like? Was it in a concert, or a rehearsal, and where? Do you remember smelling rosin in the air, or feeling a breeze in the hall? If you can recreate the other sensory details of the occasion as well, you may find it easier to pinpoint the aural portion of that memory. Check yourself on a piano or on your instrument. As time goes by, you may find that you can pull that A out of the air with increasing ease.

You don't have to stick with the A if there's another pitch that you would find easier to recreate. As a violist, it was always easy for me to audiate (hear internally, without external prompting) the opening of Bach's *Brandenburg Concerto No. 6*, an important work in the viola literature and one that begins with a strongly established Bb Major sonority. The exact pitch you choose doesn't matter. Once you've learned to accurately audiate one pitch, you can calculate your way to all others. As you practice, you will gradually learn to recognize a second pitch, and then a third, and so on.

2 Building Listening Skills

The first step toward feeling comfortable with improvisation is developing your ear. Remember, improvisation is fundamentally about listening, not playing. The more you can hear and recognize what is going on, the more comfortable you will feel.

When improvising, your hearing skills are particularly important because improvisation necessitates a sea change in how your brain and senses work together to process information. When you play a piece of printed music, your performance is the result of a series of mental and muscular processes which, though complex, is automated and familiar. First, your eyes read the notes on the page. The visual information is transmitted to your brain, which processes it and determines with lightning speed the set of muscle movements which will be necessary to produce it. Your body executes these movements, causing your instrument to produce a sound. Your ears pick up the sound and transmit the aural information back to your brain, where it is processed and evaluated.

Of course, all of this takes place so quickly that we don't really have a conscious awareness of it happening. We are so accustomed to this sequence of processes that we don't really think about it unless something goes wrong. The final arbiter of whether you have played the phrase as you intended is your sense of hearing. Your ears will tell you if your intonation was true, if the dynamics supported the shape of phrase you envisioned, or if your articulation was clean or sloppy. According to this model, the primary role of your listening skills is evaluation of the finished product.

Improvisation is built on a different idea, which requires a different series of sensory interactions. In both improvisation and performance from a score, your ears are responsible for evaluating the end result, but in improvisation they are also active at the beginning of the process, as a source for musical input. This is particularly true if you are improvising without the aid of a written-out series of chord progressions. In this case, there are no notes to read or harmonic symbols to interpret, so there is no visual input at all. Your ears must start the whole process. Instead of starting with visual information in the form of notes on a page, you must begin with aural information by hearing the sonorities and the phrase with your inner ear. It is this mental hearing of the music, the reconstruction of sounds already in your experience, that is translated into muscular impulses to produce sound on the instrument.

The upshot of all of this is that in improvisation, your ears are active participants in the music-making process, especially when you are improvising with another person. When you are asked to repeat or build on what another musician has done, you need to be able to comprehend all the nuances of your partner's phrase without relying on written notation. You must be able to recognize sequences of pitches and harmonies by ear and assimilate rhythmic patterns on one hearing.

These are advanced skills and may take you some time to master. Don't worry! In the games in this first section you will start to develop the hearing skills you will need for some of the more complex exercises later in the book. Just as you may practice an etude for several weeks to work on technical skills, you should expect that some of these hearing skills may take some time to master.

A note about musical examples: All musical examples are presented in concert pitch with the exception of works specifically composed for transposing instruments, which are presented as they normally appear. Composed works in four parts for which instrumentation is not specified are assumed to be string quartets. The top staff, in treble clef, is the first violin part; the second staff, also in treble clef, is the second violin part; the third staff, in alto clef, is the viola part; and the bottom staff, in bass clef, is the cello part. Guides to clefs are included in the appendices at the end of the book.

Pitch Switch (a game for 2, 3, or 4 players)

Begin with two players.

With eyes closed or while facing away from the others, each person simultaneously plays a long, sustained note on a pitch of his or her choosing. At a verbal command, either from one of the players or from an outside listener, each player switches to his or her partner's note.

For three players: Stand or sit in a triangle, eyes closed or facing away from each other. When the signal to switch is heard, each player should take the note of the person to his or her left side.

For four players: Sit in your usual ensemble seating, facing each other and with eyes open but taking care not to look at each other's hands (so as not to figure out the pitch by recognizing a particular finger position). Here there is the most flexibility in exchanging pitches; in a string quartet, for example, the first violin and viola could trade pitches, leaving the second violin and cello to trade with each other. Any other combination could also be used, as well as the method used in the three-player version, in which each player takes the note of the person to his or her left (or right) side.

When choosing pitches, remember to take into account the usual ranges of instruments being used. Two violinists can easily exchange notes in the upper register of the E string, but this is out of the normal range of a cellist. Similarly, a cellist playing a pitch for a violinist should keep in mind that the violin's range does not extend below the G beneath middle C; any note lower than that will require octave transposition on the part of the violinist. Although with practice both of these situations are quite navigable, they are advanced variations which should be approached after you are fluent in more usual pitch ranges.

VARIATIONS

1. Singing and playing: Try having one person sing and the other person play. If you want to make it more challenging, and your instrumental combination permits, try having each person both sing and play. The pitch switch would then involve both the sung and played pitches.

2. One-player version: If you are not a wind or brass player, you can practice this game on your own by singing one pitch and playing the other, then switching.

2. Dynamics: One partner should play loudly, one softly. Try to hear the softer pitch in spite of the louder one.

3. Duration: Instead of long, sustained notes, try short, staccato ones. Allow a few moments of silence to hear the pitches, then play the exchanged notes. For string players, try pizzicato.

Many musicians have not been asked to do this kind of work using their instruments before, and some may unexpectedly find this to be a difficult task. Musicians who have not yet learned how to relate their conception of sung pitch distance to the kinesthetic understanding of pitch relationships necessary for instrumental performance may find that they can hear their partner's pitch perfectly well but that they do not know how to get there from where they are on the instrument. This is not uncommon at the beginning of this kind of training. To work on this problem area, try the following:

Stop singing or playing your pitch for a moment, and just listen to your partner. Ask your partner to hold the pitch while you find it. The "siren" technique, in which you start at a random pitch and slowly travel up or down until you find the target pitch, is very useful for this. It is important not to do the siren too quickly, or you may pass right through the correct pitch area without realizing it. As you pass through various pitches using your siren, the relationship between your partner's fixed note and your ascending or descending notes will alternate between consonant (stable, pleasant-sounding) and dissonant (unstable, less pleasant-sounding). As you get very close to the target pitch, you will start to hear some "beats" in the sound. These beats are the sound of the wave interference produced by two frequencies that don't quite line up with one another. When you have found the pitch exactly (either as a unison or at the octave), those beats will disappear completely. Listen for this sudden clarity.

When you have found your partner's pitch, go back to your own pitch. You now know the relationship between your note and your partner's note. Go back and forth between these two notes a few times.

Now, keep your original note and ask your partner to choose a new note, one that is not very far away from the previous note. Your pitch does not change, but your partner's new note is either higher or lower than the previous one. You know where your note is, and you know where your partner's previous note was. Can you use that information to help you get a sense of where the new note is? Is it higher or lower than the previous one? Is it closer to your note, or farther away? By a lot, or by a little?

As you keep working on this, you will start to develop a sense of how far away pitches are from each other, and how those distances translate into physical sensations in your instrument, voice, and ear. Practice is essential to build this skill.

NOTES

An important element of the four-player version is that you will not be able to rely on directional hearing to figure out the pitch you need to play, since you may be trading pitches with someone across from you rather than to your left or right side. (This is somewhat less of a problem with woodwind groups, since each instrument has an easily identifiable timbre.) The issue then becomes one of communication as well as listening. How do you communicate your pitch to your intended recipient?

One way to do this is by using sound quality to make your note have a different timbre than your neighbor's. You might choose a breathy sound rather than a penetrating one, or a narrow sound rather than a broad one. Be aware of all the different timbres that you hear. Focusing on a particular quality of sound will help you isolate the pitch associated with that sound. This is the same principle that allows for differentiation of melodic vs. accompanimental voices in actual chamber music playing. Though all parts may be marked at the same dynamic level, differences in timbre and articulation can help to bring out one voice or another.

Above all, don't be so concerned with hearing your partner's note that you forget about your responsibility for communicating your own pitch. In chamber music you must be an active sender as well as an active receiver. Focus on communicating your pitch to your partner; a successful exchange depends on the clarity of your communication as well as on the listening skills of your partner.

Intervals (a game for 2, 3, or 4 players)

Only two players perform at any given time.

Sit or stand with eyes closed or while facing away from each other. Player 1 plays a long, sustained note on a pitch of his or her choosing. Player 2 listens to the pitch and joins in with the pitch that is a major third above Player 1's. Repeat, changing roles.

VARIATIONS

1. Interval: Change the interval used. You may also change the direction—for example, Player 1 may ask Player 2 to find the pitch that is a major third *below* his or her note rather than above it. Intervals of a seventh or a tritone are more challenging.

2. Duration: Use short, staccato notes rather than long, sustained ones. This makes you audiate the interval internally.

3. Speed: Player 2 should find his or her note as quickly as possible.

4. Three-player version: Player 1 plays a note. Player 3 whispers in the ear of Player 2 what the interval and direction are to be ("minor seventh down"). Player 2 performs that interval. Player 3 asks Player 1 to identify the interval and, by extension, Player 2's pitch. Rotate players among all roles. Alternatively, you can prepare slips of paper with intervals written on them and have Player 2 pick one of those slips out of a hat. Player 3 is then responsible for identifying the interval played.

5. Four-player version: As in the first three-player variant above, except that Player 4 is responsible for identifying the interval. Rotate players among all roles.

Pitch Chains (a game for 3 or more players)

Sit or stand with eyes closed or while facing away from each other. Player 1 plays a short pitch of his or her choosing. Player 2 plays the note one whole step above that. Player 3 plays the note one whole step above Player 2, and so on.

VARIATION

Change the interval used. With three players, you might decide to play the first three notes of a minor scale. With four players, the first four notes of a major or whole-tone scale. With five players, the first five notes of an octatonic scale, etc.

Sing and Play (a game for 1 player)

This game will develop your ear, your voice, and your concentration. Singers, wind players, and percussionists should use the piano for this game.

Start with a one-octave major scale in any key. Play the scale up and down in a slow tempo. While playing each note, sing the note that is a diatonic third above it. If the range of your voice is lower than that of your instrument, you will actually be singing the note that is a diatonic sixth below the sounding pitch.

EXAMPLE 2.1

EXAMPLE 2.2

VARIATIONS

1. Modality: Use a minor scale rather than a major one. Or, try whole-tone or octatonic scales.

2. Quality of the third: Instead of using the diatonic interval, sing all pitches at the interval of a major third. (What result is produced by this method?)

3. Change of interval: Sing pitches at some other interval relative to the played note. Thirds and sixths are the easiest intervals to hear, followed by perfect fourths and fifths. Seconds, sevenths, and tritones are the most challenging.

4. Dual direction: While playing the upward scale, start your singing voice on the upper tonic and sing the scale downward. Watch out for the upward fa–sol and downward sol–fa degrees; changing between these two notes will require the same skills as the one-person variant of the "Pitch Switch" game.

5. Arpeggios: Use a one-octave arpeggio instead of a scale. The sung pitches should be the next adjacent pitches within the arpeggio. If you want to practice a more complicated arpeggio pattern, see the example below.

EXAMPLE 2.3. To be performed as a canon between voice and instrument, at the rhythmic interval of one note.

This pattern involves several different arpeggios that all have a note in common (in this case, C). After several different arpeggios that start on C, the pattern modulates to the key of F, and the whole series can begin again using arpeggios that all have F in common. Analyze the chords below the staff using Roman numerals or letter names to show the root, quality, and inversion of each chord.

The best way to practice this more complicated set of arpeggios is to make a canon with yourself by singing and playing. In this canon, the voice and the instrument should be separated by one note. If you begin by playing the first C on the piano, then when you play the next note, E♭, the voice comes in on the C you just left. Then the piano moves on to the G while the voice sings the E♭.

For a greater challenge, start by leading with the singing voice and following with the instrument. The moments at which the chords change are especially challenging and require you to hear the new chord sonority in advance.

More Sing and Play (a game for 1 player on any instrument)

This one works for players of any instrument. As before, singers should use the piano.

Choose a major or minor scale, one octave. Go up and down the scale, alternating played notes with sung ones. This requires physical coordination and concentration as well as a good ear. Both voice and fingers must be following along internally so that you are always ready to produce the right note. Be especially careful if you are singing in a different register than you are playing, particularly if you are singing in a lower octave than your instrument. In this case, the sounding intervals will be the inversions of the intervals on the page.

EXAMPLE 2.4

EXAMPLE 2.5

VARIATIONS

1. Rhythmic pattern: Execute the scale in some rhythmic pattern rather than using all long notes.

2. Substitution of rests/claps for designated pitches: Make it a rule that you will never sing or play a particular note. For example, if you choose the note *mi*, then whenever you have a mi, substitute a rest. Jump back in with the next note, singing or playing as appropriate. When you've mastered that, take out an additional note. You can substitute a clap or a foot tap for the missing notes if you like.

Advanced Sing and Play (a game for 1 string or piano player)

Here, the previous game is carried to its logical next step.

Perform the following examples, playing one line and singing the other. Transpose octaves as necessary for your voice or instrumental range.

EXAMPLE 2.6

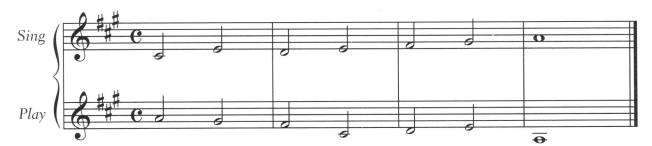

EXAMPLE 2.7

EXAMPLE 2.8

Reverse parts at will. For a greater challenge, switch playing and singing every bar or two during the exercise. For further practice, use duets from sight-singing or ear-training texts, or choose simple instrumental duets with singable melodic or bass lines.

One Third Plus One Third Equals One Fifth
(a game for 3 or 4 players)

For three players: Stand or sit in a triangle, closing eyes or facing away from each other. Player 1 plays or sings a sustained note of his or her choosing. Player 2 plays or sings a pitch that is a major third above Player 1's. Player 3 joins in with a pitch that is a minor third above Player 2's, so that a major triad is created with Player 1's note as the root.

For four players: Players 1, 2, and 3 as above. Player 4 joins in with a

pitch that is a minor third above Player 3's, so that a dominant seventh chord is created (again with Player 1's note as the root).

Change the quality of the target chord (major, minor, augmented, or diminished), and adjust the intervals accordingly. For example, in a three-person game, if the chord quality is augmented, Player 1 chooses a pitch, Player 2 plays a major third above Player 1, and Player 3 plays a major third above Player 2. You can write the available chord qualities on slips of paper and pull them out of a hat to make sure they come out randomly.

For a four-person game, you can explore all kinds of commonly used seventh chords (major, minor, dominant, half-diminished, and fully diminished). Need a refresher in seventh chords? Turn to appendix A in the back of the book.

Getting to the Root of the Problem (a game for 3 or 4 players)

This is similar to the previous game, but requires more advanced hearing skills.

For three players: Player 1 plays or sings a sustained note on a pitch of his or her choosing. Player 1 announces the position of his or her note (root, third, or fifth) in a triad. For example, Player 1 might play the note F♯ and say, "This is the third of a major triad." The other players fill in the remaining notes of the triad (in this case, D and A). Player 1 should never say the name of his or her note; all interval calculations are to be performed by ear. When all the notes are sounding, identify which player has the root of the chord.

For four players: Player 1 as above, except that he or she will be choosing the position of his or her note in a seventh chord (for example, "This note is the fifth of a half-diminished seventh chord"). Players 2, 3, and 4 fill in the remaining notes one at a time. When all notes are sounding, identify which player has the root of the chord.

VARIATIONS FOR EITHER VERSION

Player 1 plays or sings a note, without specifying its place in any chord. Player 2 chooses a note at the interval of a third (major or minor) either above or below Player 1's note. Player 3 then chooses a note at the interval of a third (major or minor) away from either Player 1 or Player 2. Once all the notes are sounding, identify the quality of the resultant chord (major, minor, augmented, diminished) and determine who has the root. Example: Player 1 plays a B♭. Player 2 plays a minor third below Player 1 (G). Player 3 plays a major third above Player 1 (D). The resultant chord is minor in quality, and its root is Player 2's note.

The variation is the same for the four-player version, but the permutations are more numerous. Example: Player 1 chooses an A. Player 2 plays an F (a major third below Player 1). Player 3 plays a D (a minor third below Player 2). Player 4 plays a C (a minor third above Player 1). The resultant chord is a mm7 chord, and the root is Player 2's D. Warning: You may occasionally end up with chords outside the realm of common practice harmony! See if you can figure out what kinds of seventh chords these might be, and why they are not commonly used.

Sound Effects (a game for 2 or 4 players)

Begin with two players.

Player 1: Stand in the center of the floor. Improvise a single movement or a short series of movements that you can repeat without tiring. Use your whole body, not just your arms and hands. Repeat the movement over and over.

Player 2: Observe Player 1's movement carefully. Think about how his or her movement could be represented using sound. When you are ready, play your musical accompaniment to his or her movement. Try to represent the movement in as much detail as possible.

This is a free-form improvisation in which the goal is to produce "sounds" rather than "pitches." Do not aim for a structured representation with a melody or any specific pitches—only try to represent the quality of Player 1's movement in sound. For example, if Player 1 falls to the floor, Player 2 might accompany that with a glissando. A trembling motion might be represented by a trill or by tremolo playing or flutter-tonguing. The goal is to think outside the confines of melodies and harmonies to experiment with gestures in sound. You may want to use your instrument and voice simultaneously, or to add a foot tap or other kinds of body percussion.

After a while, switch roles.

For four players: Players 1 and 2 begin as in the two-player version. After they have established their movement and sound, Player 3 should join Player 1 and improvise a contrasting movement. Player 4 must represent Player 3's movement in sound. If Players 1 and 3 decide to interact with each other in a kind of movement "conversation," Players 2 and 4 should follow with their sound effects. Change roles.

Listen carefully to the sound effects of the accompanying players. Do they accurately represent the way that the movements interact? How might this exercise relate to "real" ensemble playing?

Rhythmic Scales (a game for 2, 3, or 4 players)

In this game, players will improvise rhythmic patterns for each other to imitate, using the familiar notes of the one-octave major or minor scale. Dalcroze Eurhythmics teacher Herb Henke uses this exercise for beginning piano improvisation. Some extra twists are added here to create a multi-player game.

As a group, decide on which scale to use first, and pick a meter. Player 1 will play an ascending one-octave scale in a rhythm of his or her choosing. The scale should last for two complete bars, and you must use all of the time within those two bars.

At the downbeat of the third bar, Player 2 enters, playing the same ascending scale in the same rhythm that Player 1 just established. Meanwhile, Player 1 plays the descending version of the scale in the same rhythmic pattern (or continues playing the scale upward into a second octave). This will indicate whether Player 2 has heard the pattern correctly.

EXAMPLE 2.9

It is now Player 2's turn to lead with a new rhythmic pattern.

VARIATIONS

1. Tonality: When it comes time for the cycle to start over, choose a different scale, or change from major to minor mode. Depending on the listening skills of the players, this change can either be improvised on the spot or announced just slightly ahead of time.

2. Meter: The person starting a new scale may, in addition to changing the tonality, change the meter. Announce the change of meter so the responding player can follow without confusion.

3. Sing and Play: This game can be effectively combined with the "More Sing and Play" exercise from earlier in the chapter. Player 1 can execute the scale by alternately singing and playing. For an even greater challenge, you can combine this exercise with the original "Sing and Play" game in which you sing a fixed-interval line above or below the played scale. Player 2 would be responsible for duplicating Player 1's sung line as well as the played one.

4. Modality: Use modes rather than major or minor scales, or use whole-tone or octatonic scales. The example below uses a whole-tone scale.

EXAMPLE 2.10

3 Simple Melodic Improvisations

In this section, you will create simple one- or two-line improvisations starting with the common building blocks of scales and arpeggios. You will also start to experiment with simple rhythmic and motivic variation and with melodic improvisations outside the realm of common-practice harmony.

In the second chapter, in which you worked primarily with pitch relationships, you were not required to conform to a particular meter or work with set rhythmic values until the very last game. From this point onward, we will be adding rhythmic and metric constraints to your improvisations, because rhythm is vitally important in creating direction in a phrase. Of course, the more balls there are to juggle, the easier it is to drop one, and having to improvise a melody that conforms to a specified metric structure can present unexpected challenges. These challenges usually manifest in one of two ways: either players are concentrating so hard on what pitches to choose that they lose their sense of pulse and the rhythm founders, or they are so conscious of each passing beat that they become paralyzed and it becomes difficult for them to be spontaneous and creative. No matter what happens, whether what comes out of your instrument is what you intended or not, always keep the integrity of the underlying pulse. This will require some self-control, since the temptation to stop and "fix things" is very strong. Think of yourself as a beginning surfer: your goal at first is simply to stay on the board and learn to keep your balance while different things are going on. As you become more experienced, you will have more control over what you are doing. Tasks that seem to require all your attention right now will eventually become automated and easy.

Both here and in the following chapters, musical excerpts from real pieces are presented as examples. Rather than just looking at these excerpts, you are encouraged to play them through in whatever way you can: with your ensemble, at the piano, etc., so that you experience the examples aurally and kinesthetically as well as visually.

Sugar and Spice and Everything Nice
(That's What Melodies Are Made of)

EXAMPLE 3.1. Mozart: Overture to *Le Nozze di Figaro* (Presto)

One of the biggest stumbling blocks that many beginning improvisers face is creating a melody, because many of us try to make melodies that are too complicated. If you study the literature, you will find that many of the most beautiful melodies by great composers are not complicated at all, and are largely made up of two elemental building blocks: scales and arpeggios.

Here are some melodies that are mostly composed of scales or fragments of scales:

EXAMPLE 3.2. Haydn (attributed): "St. Anthony" Chorale (Andante)

EXAMPLE 3.3. Beethoven: Symphony No. 9 (*Choral*), 4th mvt. (Allegro assai)

EXAMPLE 3.4. Mouret: Rondeau (Moderato)

EXAMPLE 3.5. Beethoven: Concerto for Violin and Orchestra, 1st mvt. (Allegro ma non troppo)

Scalar motion by itself can get monotonous quickly. The arpeggio is a good way to get from one part of the scale to another. Here are some melodies that are made up mostly of arpeggios:

EXAMPLE 3.6. Mozart: Serenade, K. 525 (*Eine Kleine Nachtmusik*), 1st mvt. (Allegro)

EXAMPLE 3.7. Schubert: Symphony No. 5, 3rd mvt. (Menuetto)

EXAMPLE 3.8. Beethoven: Symphony No. 3 (*Eroica*), 1st mvt. (Allegro con brio)

EXAMPLE 3.9. Prokofiev: "Montagues and Capulets" from *Romeo and Juliet* (Allegro pesante)

EXAMPLE 3.10. Strauss, Johann (Jr.): "An der schönen blauen Donau" (Tempo di Valse)

Combining scale fragments with arpeggios creates many melodic possibilities:

EXAMPLE 3.11. Mozart: Serenade, K. 525 (*Eine Kleine Nachtmusik*), 2nd mvt. (Romance: Andante)

EXAMPLE 3.12. Purcell: Rondeau (theme from Britten's *Young Person's Guide to the Orchestra*) (Allegro)

EXAMPLE 3.13. Mozart: Piano Concerto No. 21, K. 467 (*Elvira Madigan*), 2nd mvt. (Andante)

EXAMPLE 3.14. Schubert: Symphony No. 8 in b minor (*Unfinished*), 1st mvt. (Allegro moderato)

EXAMPLE 3.15. Tchaikovsky: *Swan Lake*, Act II: Scene (Moderato)

Of course, not every melody is composed this way. But if you feel timid about creating your own melodies, you can always rely on familiar scale fragments and arpeggios to get you through.

Great melodies are generally very singable, even if they weren't originally composed for the voice. Instrumentalists tend to naturally approach improvisation and composition from the vantage point of their instruments, and tend to view what's possible and desirable in a melody through the lens of the technical idiosyncrasies of those instruments. Instead, try thinking about singing your melody before playing it. You may be able to leap suddenly from one register to another on your instrument, but if you can't do it with your voice, it's probably not a good technique to use regularly in building a melody. Think of things like sudden register changes and awkward intervals as special effects, to be used very sparingly and in just the right places. Aim for a melody line that is smooth and singable overall, using more unusual musical ideas to highlight one or two crucial moments.

When improvising melodies for most of the games in this book, start with the proportions of a lot of sugar to a little spice. In other words, your melodies should be mostly scalar or arpeggio-based with one or two surprises thrown in. These surprises could be an unusual interval, the use of a few chromatic notes, a sudden register change, etc. Melodies that have too many unusual features don't hang together well as a unit. An example of a melody that incorporates all of these aspects is the well-known theme of Elgar's *Pomp and Circumstance* March No. 1, from which a portion is excerpted below:

EXAMPLE 3.16. Elgar: *Pomp and Circumstance March No. 1* (Largamente)

These suggestions are by no means hard-and-fast rules, but they are good guidelines for exploration when you are just beginning. Once you are comfortable improvising your own melodies, you may want to try pushing these boundaries a little.

Fast-Forward (a game for 2 players)

This game combines simple melodic improvisations with quick-response and listening skills.

1. Together, choose a one-octave scale. The only notes you are allowed to use in this improvisation are the eight notes of that scale. If you find that too limiting, you may extend the scale an extra three notes on the bottom by including scale degrees 5, 6, and 7 beneath the original tonic.

2. Start in $\frac{4}{4}$ meter in a slow tempo (no faster than ♩ = 60 to start with). Player 1 will improvise a simple pattern, always beginning on the tonic of the chosen scale. This pattern will last one complete bar. Immediately after Player 1 finishes, Player 2 will repeat Player 1's pattern exactly twice as fast (as if it were written in $\frac{4}{8}$ rather than $\frac{4}{4}$).

3. Without pause, Player 1 improvises a new pattern. The goal is a seamless transition between $\frac{4}{4}$ and $\frac{4}{8}$ bars. See the example below:

EXAMPLE 3.17

EXAMPLE 3.17 *Continued*

Here Player 2 must keep track of both pitch and rhythm. The reason for starting each of Player 1's bars on the tonic is so that if Player 2 has trouble repeating the melody, he or she can recoup at the next bar, knowing that it will always begin on the tonic note. As you become more advanced, you may wish to discard this rule and allow melodies to start on any pitch.

Keep the melodic patterns simple at first; this game is aimed at quick-response skills, not dictation. Expand the range of notes you use as your listening skills develop.

VARIATIONS

1. Chromaticism: As your listening skills develop, try adding chromaticism—or, use whole-tone or octatonic scales.

2. Augmentation: In this variation, Player 2 repeats Player 1's melody twice as slowly rather than twice as quickly. For this version, the original tempo should be on the fast side.

3. Meter: Experiment with different meters. Some are easier than others; for example, $\frac{3}{4}$ ($\frac{3}{8}$) is more straightforward than $\frac{5}{4}$ ($\frac{5}{8}$). If you choose a meter with fewer beats in each bar, such as $\frac{3}{4}$, you may wish to extend the length of the improvisation to two bars at a time.

He Says, She Says (a game for 2, 3, or 4 players)

This is a very simple exercise in antecedent-consequent phrasing.

Begin with two players.

Together, decide on a tonality and a meter. Play the scale of the tonality or a tonic chord to get the tonal center firmly in your ear.

Player 1 improvises a simple, short (two-bar) melody that begins on the tonic degree. The end of this melody should be any scale degree other than 1.

Player 2 answers with a similar two-bar melody that starts on any scale degree other than 1 and cadences to the tonic. You might begin on the same note with which Player 1 ended, or you may start somewhere else in the scale. The goal is to pick up motivic elements from Player 1's melody and use them in your answer.

Keep your melodies simple. Using scalar motion is a good way to get started. As your listening and improvisational skills develop, add arpeggiated motion or an occasional chromatic note. This is not an exercise in making up the most virtuosic melody you can think of. Remember, someone else must respond to what you play. Just like a spoken conversation, a musical conversation works best when both parties can participate equally.

EXAMPLE 3.18

EXAMPLE 3.19

For three players: Players 1 and 2 begin as above, each improvising a two-bar phrase, except that Player 2's melody cadences to scale degree 5, not 1. Player 3 then improvises a four-bar phrase which makes a suitable connection with where Player 2 left off and gets back to the tonic. See the example below:

EXAMPLE 3.20

EXAMPLE 3.20 *Continued*

For four players: Players 1 and 2 begin as above. At the conclusion of Player 2's phrase, Player 3 repeats Player 1's melody in the minor mode (or major if the original was minor), and Player 4 repeats Player 2's answer in the minor mode.

VARIATIONS

1. Meter: In addition to the common meters of $\frac{4}{4}$, $\frac{3}{4}$, $\frac{6}{8}$, $\frac{9}{8}$, and $\frac{12}{8}$, try improvising in $\frac{5}{4}$ and $\frac{7}{4}$. Or, alternate bars of two different time signatures: $\frac{3}{4} + \frac{3}{8}$, $\frac{12}{8} + \frac{3}{2}$, or $\frac{5}{4} + \frac{4}{4}$.

2. Phrase length: Try improvising four bars at a time instead of just two. In the three-player version, Player 3 would then have to improvise eight bars instead of four.

Rhythm in an Alternate Universe (a game for 4 or more players)

It is often illuminating and useful to look at pieces being studied and think about what they would have been like if the composers had made different choices about fundamental elements like meter and modality. Making a simple alteration such as changing the meter of a work can totally transform our sense of phrasing, direction, and energy. For example, Bach wrote the following well-known piece as a minuet, in $\frac{3}{4}$ time:

EXAMPLE 3.21

In 1965, the pop group The Toys created their own version of the song using Bach's melody and harmony, but in $\frac{4}{4}$ time. The melody from their version, called "A Lover's Concerto," is below:

EXAMPLE 3.22

SIMPLE MELODIC IMPROVISATIONS

Sometimes composers themselves cannot decide which meter better suits their musical ideas. For example, Handel created two versions of the aria "Rejoice greatly" from *Messiah*. One version is in $\frac{6}{8}$, one in $\frac{4}{4}$. Excerpts from each appear below; observe the way in which Handel changed the note values to accommodate each meter.

EXAMPLE 3.23

EXAMPLE 3.24

EXAMPLE 3.25.
Mozart, Sinfonia Concertante for Violin, Viola, and Orchestra, K. 364, 2nd mvt. (Andante)

Imagining how things might have been written in an alternate universe is always a fun game to play. It sometimes yields startling results, as in the next example, based on the second movement of Mozart's Sinfonia Concertante for Violin and Viola, K. 364. The opening theme is reproduced below with a reduced version of the orchestral accompaniment. Play through the example.

Solo
Violin

Orchestra

In an alternate universe, however, Mozart might have written this as a dance movement—for example, a tango.

EXAMPLE 3.26

Play through this version as well. Observe how the accompaniment patterns have been altered to heighten the rhythmic qualities of the tango.

You can try this technique with any piece you're currently working on. This is a great way to develop quick-response rhythmic skills. You might start with simply changing a binary meter to a ternary one, such as $\frac{4}{4}$ to $\frac{12}{8}$,

$\frac{2}{4}$ to $\frac{6}{8}$, or $\frac{3}{4}$ to $\frac{9}{8}$. Later, you can change pieces written in $\frac{3}{4}$ to $\frac{4}{4}$ (in which case you will have to stretch the material out to cover an extra beat) or $\frac{4}{4}$ to $\frac{3}{4}$ (in which case you will need to compress the material into a shorter bar). Don't try to do this throughout a whole movement at first; just choose a section of sixteen bars or so for practice.

There is an old saying, "familiarity breeds contempt"; or, the more we become familiar with something (or someone), the more we tend to take it for granted. Playing a piece in a different meter is a great way to wake up your ears and brain and make the piece fresh again, so that when you return it to the original meter you are really hearing it rather than taking it for granted.

Music Plus One (a game for 1 player plus recording)

If you are interested in practicing melodic improvisation by yourself, here's one way to do it. Get a recording of the Pachelbel Canon in D, preferably one in which the tempo is on the slow side. The advantage to using this piece is that it is made up of one harmonic progression repeated over and over. The harmonic progression is as follows:

EXAMPLE 3.27

Analyze the progression, writing the Roman numerals under the staff.

Play along with the recording, making up your own melody. Since the phrase repeats every two bars, you will have plenty of chances to try different styles, textures, dynamics, registers, etc. And since you are not playing with anyone else, feel free to try new and daring things—chromaticism, passing tones, appoggiaturas, etc. This is a great way to experiment with melodic improvisation on your own and to build confidence in your abilities.

Mosaic (a game for 2 or more players)

Although this is a simple game, it deals with one of the most intricate subtleties of musicianship: how to combine the fragmented parts of a melody so that a single idea is presented.

Take a look at the following musical examples:

EXAMPLE 3.28. Beethoven: String Quartet in E♭ Major, Op. 74 (*Harp*), 1st. mvt. (Allegro)

EXAMPLE 3.28 *Continued*

EXAMPLE 3.29. Tchaikovsky: String Quartet No. 1 in D Major, Op. 11, 4th mvt. (Finale: Allegro giusto)

EXAMPLE 3.30. Beethoven: String Quartet in c♯ minor, Op. 131, 5th mvt. (Presto)

In each of these examples, a line has been spread out over several voices. The parts must be played in such a way that the integrity of the whole line is preserved without jarring entrances and exits. Although these excerpts are all taken from chamber music, the same technique appears in works from various other genres as well. As you see from the above excerpts, sometimes the line is constructed so that there is an overlap of entrance and exit, sometimes not.

1. Choose a melody. You can write one of your own, or use an existing melody that everyone in your group knows. I have provided several here in hopes that you'll find at least one that all the members of your ensemble can play in the same octave. If the instruments in your ensemble are widely different in range, you may wish to play this game in a series of rounds (not in the canonic sense!), with two or three instruments of similar range playing together.

EXAMPLE 3.31. Bach: *Brandenburg Concerto No. 2*, 3rd mvt. (Allegro assai) (adapted)

EXAMPLE 3.32. Schubert: String Quartet in a minor (*Rosamund*), 1st mvt. (Allegro ma non troppo)

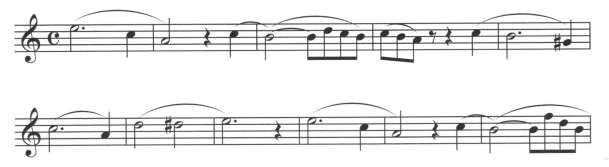

EXAMPLE 3.32 *Continued*

EXAMPLE 3.33. Mozart: String Quartet in A Major, K. 464, 1st. mvt. (Allegro)

EXAMPLE 3.34. Mozart: Horn Quintet, K. 407, 2nd mvt. (Andante)

2. Play the melody once all together so everyone has it in his or her ears.

3. You will be performing this melody by breaking it up into small parts and trading those parts back and forth. Choose one person to be the starting player. From that person, you will go around your group either clockwise or counterclockwise, as you like. Divide the melody among all players. You might want to start by switching from one person to another at the bar line, but a more challenging way to do this is by choosing a number of beats for each person that is *not* the same as the number of beats in the bar. For example, if you are playing the Schubert example, in $\frac{3}{4}$, you might have players switch every two beats. This creates a more interesting overlap of fragments and helps avoid the unintentional accents on the downbeats that often occur when rotation among players happens at the bar line.

In order to make the various fragments sound like they are all part of one line, you must feel the direction of the whole line at all times, especially when you are not playing. Not only must you match the other players in terms of dynamics, articulation, sound quality, and quality of attack, you must remember where your fragment lies in terms of the direction of the overall phrase. Does your fragment fall within a crescendo that adds direction to the phrase? If so, at what dynamic level will you start and finish? Take the line from the person who played before you and give it to the person who plays after you. Breaking the line up into such short fragments means your attention will be constantly focused on the connection between players, not on any one person's ownership of the melody.

Play the melody through in pieces several times, trying to make it sound like one line.

4. Play the melody in pieces again, with your eyes closed. Is it easier or more difficult to create the line? Is the quality of your sound affected? What about your level of communication with others? Have one player sit out and listen objectively to the two versions, eyes opened and eyes closed. Is there a difference?

VARIATIONS

1. Length of fragment: Experiment with fragments that are both longer and shorter than the length of a bar. Or, change after a given number of notes (regardless of how many beats those notes occupy). You also need not start your fragments on the beat; they might begin on the half-beat or on the second sixteenth note of each beat, for instance. (This is particularly true of melodies that begin with pickups.)

2. Fragment pyramid: For a real brainteaser, create a series of fragments of different lengths. In a four-person group, the first person might play one beat of the melody, the second two, the third three, and the fourth four. Remember, the goal is not just to keep your place, but to play musically.

Keep Away (a game for 4 or more players, or 1 player plus piano)

This is an easy way to practice making up a melody within a given harmony.

EXAMPLE 3.35

1. Below is a transcription of the traditional Irish folk song "Cockles and Mussels." Play it through once as written. In a four-player game,

FROM SIGHT TO SOUND

Player 1 plays the melody, Player 2 the harmony, and Player 3 the bass line (double parts if necessary). Player 4 is silent for the first play-through.

2. Notate the harmony under the staff. What chords does it contain?

3. Play the piece again. This time, Player 1 is silent and Player 4 must create a new melody, "keeping away" from the original. The new melody must never coincide with the old melody—you may never have the same note at the same time as the original melody. Use the chord symbols to help you figure out what your available notes are. You don't have to use the same rhythm as the original melody (in fact, it will be better if you don't). Use whatever rhythmic combinations you like.

4. When you reach the end, immediately repeat, adding Player 1 with the original melody. Do the original melody and the countermelody work together?

In the one-player-plus-piano version, the piano is responsible for bass line, harmony, and the original melody, while the other player is responsible for the countermelody.

You can apply this technique to almost any piece in which there is a clear melody/accompaniment relationship. Folk songs and children's songs are easy to work with because they are short, the harmony is generally simple, and there are no severe technical demands, but you may also enjoy creating "keep away" countermelodies for great tunes from the orchestral, operatic, or chamber music repertoire.

Fill in the Blank (a game for 4 or more players)

Here is an opportunity for each of you to practice improvising very short segments while playing as a group. Below are three examples from real chamber music literature. One is a string quartet, one a woodwind quintet, and one a brass quintet. Choose whichever one is closest to the instrumentation of your group.

You will notice that certain bars have been blanked out and marked with a question mark in each of the parts at different times. Play through the excerpt once as it is. Then play through it again, improvising in the bars with question marks. (There are other bars of rest that do not have question marks over them; these rests have been written in by the composer and it is not necessary to improvise during these bars.) Try to stay within the style of the piece and fit into the harmony as well as you can. After you have improvised, turn the page to the complete version and see what the composer actually did.

If you find it too challenging to have all of the parts filling in blanks at the same time, start by having only one or two players playing from the incomplete version and the rest from the complete version. This will limit the amount of improvising going on at any given moment.

You can do this exercise with virtually any piece of music, and it's excellent practice. Just photocopy the score and blank out a bar or two at a time.

EXAMPLE 3.36. Haydn: String Quartet in g minor, Op. 74, No. 3 (*The Riders*), 3rd mvt. (Menuetto)

EXAMPLE 3.36. *Continued*

EXAMPLE 3.37. Danzi: Quintet for Winds in B♭ Major, Op. 56, No. 1, 1st mvt. (Allegretto)

EXAMPLE 3.37 *Continued*

EXAMPLE 3.38. William Boyce: Suite (transcribed by Howard Cable), 4th mvt. (Moderato)

Trumpet in B♭ (or picc.)

Trumpet in B♭

Horn in F

Trombone

Tuba

EXAMPLE 3.38 *Continued*

The composers' original versions can be found here:

EXAMPLE 3.39. Haydn: String Quartet in g minor, Op. 74, No. 3 (*The Riders*), 3rd mvt. (Menuetto)

EXAMPLE 3.39 *Continued*

EXAMPLE 3.40. Danzi: Quintet for Winds in B♭ Major, Op. 56, No. 1, 1st mvt. (Allegretto)

EXAMPLE 3.40 *Continued*

EXAMPLE 3.41. William Boyce: Suite (transcribed by Howard Cable), 4th mvt. (Moderato)

Trumpet
in B♭
(or picc.)

Trumpet
in B♭

Horn in F

Trombone

Tuba

EXAMPLE 3.41 *Continued*

Non-Tonal Improvisations

The next few games deal with improvisation outside the chord-based environment of common practice harmony. Although they are called "non-tonal," these exercises still use organizing principles related to tonal concepts, but they do not include traditional triads or chords. For some people, removing the restrictions of harmonic practice is freeing, while for others, the loss of that reassuring structure and sense of "home" can cause anxiety. You will get many chances in this book to improvise within harmonic guidelines, so take this opportunity to break out of the mold. This will benefit your improvisational skills by allowing you to see what kinds of pitch relationships are possible when you are allowed to use *all* the crayons in the box. Additionally, working with non-tonal improvisations will help you feel more comfortable when you are back improvising within a harmonic setting.

All of the examples included use melodies that came out of actual improvisation sessions. I have transcribed them here to show you that these melodies are sometimes not "perfect" from a compositional sense, but that doesn't matter at all. By analyzing what's not "perfect" about our melodies, we get a better mental picture of the stylistic and aural palette we are aiming for, and it helps us refine our ears and our choices for the next time around.

Strings Alone (a game for 2, 3, or 4 players, mostly strings)

This is a free-form improvisation without harmonic requirements. It is meant to encourage experimentation in freely improvised melody. The basic rules are the same regardless of the number of players.

With a little creativity, this game is easily adapted for non-string groups. The piano is a particularly helpful instrument to include here.

1. Choose one person to improvise a melody, and choose a meter for your improvisation.
2. The other players, all string players, will set up an ostinato rhythmic pattern using only open strings, either one string at a time or in double stops. Keep the rhythmic patterns minimalist in texture, since they are meant to support the melody. Examples of possible ostinati are shown below:

EXAMPLE 3.42

3. Once the ostinato is going, the melody player may improvise a free line over it. Don't worry about creating a phrase, conforming to a key, etc.—just play around with the pitches and see what you like. Use the ostinato to help you maintain a rhythmic pulse, but don't let it define your improvisation. Because there aren't any rules to which you must conform, there's no such thing as a "mistake." When you've had enough, stop playing the melody and play an open-string ostinato. This will signal that it's someone else's turn to take over.

EXAMPLE 3.43

Don't worry about whether it sounds classical enough, or jazzy enough, or "right" or "wrong." The point of this game is just to listen to how pitches sound next to each other. Don't try to plan it out beforehand— just start playing and see what comes out.

Since we spend so much time in our practicing trying to get things exactly right, we often have the tendency to try to stop and "fix things" when what comes out of the instrument isn't exactly what we wanted. It takes a lot of discipline to sit with notes that didn't sound the way you thought they would and just let them be, calmly and without any little moments of anxiety. This game gives you a great opportunity to practice creating without judgment.

Drone (a game for 2 string players, or 3 non–string players)

This game requires a different number of players for its string and non-string versions because again, sustained intervals are required in the accompaniment. The basic rules are the same in both versions.

Not all music is harmonically complicated. Some pieces are made up of just a few ideas. This is particularly true of folk songs. Take a look at the example below, which is the "Pe Loc" movement from Bartók's *Rumanian Folk Dances* for small orchestra:

EXAMPLE 3.44. Bartók: *Rumanian Folk Dances*, for small orchestra, 3rd mvt. ("Pe Loc") (Andante)

There are just a few elements to this piece. The melody is made up of notes within a particular scale (here, the F♯ harmonic minor scale), and the harmony is just a few sustained intervals. (The complete orchestration contains some gentle arpeggiation of the intervals as well.) Rhythmically, the piece is made up of a handful of short motives that repeat throughout.

STRING VERSION

Player 1 will play the melody and Player 2 the accompaniment.

1. Together, choose a tonal center and a meter.
2. Player 2 should choose two different intervals, which will make up the harmony for your improvisation. In Bartók's example, and in the example reproduced below, the two intervals chosen are a fifth and a sixth. You will combine these intervals to form a "non-harmonic progression." For your first attempts, you may wish to agree with Player 1 on a phrase structure, such as two bars tonic, two bars non-tonic, two bars tonic, one bar non-tonic, one bar tonic.

As you become more advanced, however, you can abandon an organized structure and do your improvisations by ear, communicating your intention to change "harmony" to your partner by sound quality and body language.

3. Player 2 should begin playing his or her pattern in long sustained notes, one bow per bar. If you are using a preordained structure you can do this as an ostinato pattern.

4. Player 1 will improvise a melody over these alternating intervals. You are restricted to using only the notes in the minor scale based on your tonal center. The choice of drone intervals may affect which minor scale you choose! Since the accompaniment texture is really a drone, you are quite free to use any texture you like. Borrow Bartók's idea of combining a few rhythmic patterns to make a phrase.

EXAMPLE 3.45

Listen carefully to the sound of different intervals against the drone. When you find a note that is dissonant, play it with confidence! Lean into the dissonance and really see what it feels like; without the tension that dissonance creates, there is no corresponding sense of release in resolution.

Since Player 2 has the "harmony," he or she is largely in control of the phrase length and direction. This is true even though only two sonorities are being used. Experiment with ways to combine your two intervals to produce different phrase lengths and directions. When you are experienced with using two intervals, you may add a third one. Think carefully about the role that this third sonority will play. Do you want it to serve as a kind of subdominant? Dominant? How will its use affect the role of the other two sonorities, and how will you use it to shape your phrase?

Switch roles when you are ready.

VARIATIONS FOR THE NON-STRING VERSION

If you are playing instruments that cannot produce simultaneous fifths, you will need to have more structure. The accompaniment will have to be produced by Players 2 and 3 working in tandem on a previously agreed-upon pattern of tonic and non-tonic intervals, as in the above example.

VARIATIONS FOR BOTH VERSIONS

1. Ostinati: Instead of playing the harmonies as sustained intervals, you might arpeggiate them using an ostinato pattern.

2. Melodic construction: Instead of a harmonic minor scale, use a pentatonic, modal, whole-tone, or octatonic scale as melodic material. You may need to vary the quality of the drone interval if you want it to fit in with your scale; for example, a perfect fifth isn't found within a whole-tone scale, so your drone intervals might be tritones or any major interval.

Snake (a game for 2 players)

Like the Drone game, this exercise involves putting a melody over a non-harmonic repetitive pattern.

Player 1 will play the melody, Player 2 the accompaniment. Together, choose a meter for your improvisation.

1. Player 2 should pick two sets of minor seconds, to be played melodically in eighth notes. For example: E–F and B–C.

As in the Drone game, these are the two sonorities that will determine the tonic center. Combine these two patterns in any order you like. At first, do not change sonorities within the bar; when both players are comfortable, you may occasionally change the "harmonic rhythm" of the sonorities by changing halfway through the bar.

2. Player 1's job is to improvise a melody over these repeated eighth notes. Longer note values are likely to be more successful in this exercise since the accompaniment pattern is made up of shorter notes. The material for the melody can come from any scale that includes the two patterns Player 2 has chosen. In the above example, Player 1 could build a melody on material from the C Major, A minor (harmonic is most color-

ful), G Mixolydian, D Dorian, or E Phrygian scales (as well as several others), since all these scales contain B, C, E, and F. Each of these scales will produce a melody with a different color. How well you build your melody will determine how successful you are at convincing the listener of your tonal center.

EXAMPLE 3.46

If you like, you can just keep switching back and forth between these two sonorities over and over so that you really get to hear how different pitches sound when played against these ostinati. Or, you could decide to make your improvisation last a set number of bars, and you could try to alternate between the two ostinati in a way that sets up a sense of phrasing. In this case you might want to make the last bar just a sustained drone note so that you have a sense of finishing the phrase.

Switch roles when you are ready.

VARIATIONS

1. Sonority: Use major seconds instead of minor, or one of each. Or, use minor or major thirds.

2. Quick response: At a prearranged musical signal, switch roles without letting the accompaniment eighth notes falter. Keep the same two sets of minor seconds.

3. Meter: The non-tonal games are particularly interesting when non-traditional meters are used. Experiment with $\frac{5}{8}$, $\frac{7}{8}$, and alternating bars of more traditional meters ($\frac{6}{8}$ and $\frac{4}{8}$, etc.).

4 Melody and Harmony: Improvisations for Ensembles

You now have all the tools you need to improvise as a group and create a real piece of music complete with melody, bass line, and harmony.

When you improvise alone, you are in charge of all aspects of the music. When multiple people are improvising simultaneously, some ground rules are needed to prevent total chaos. Here, those ground rules take the form of a harmonic progression, which will form the basis of your improvisation. The sample chord progressions are suitable for all or almost all of the exercises, so if you would like to repeat a game using a different progression, simply borrow one from one of the surrounding pages. An additional collection of progressions for improvisation appears in appendix B at the end of this book.

In this section, the progressions are given using chords that have been realized in four voices. Play from the music first, and then once you are comfortable with the sound of the progression, try to play from memory, identifying each chord by its sonority, not by the written notes on the page. You will need to be able to identify each sonority with a Roman numeral or otherwise identify its function. In chapter 5, you will begin to make the transition to improvising without the benefit of written-out progressions, so if you can start learning these skills now, you will have a head start.

Do not rush through this chapter. Chapter 4 is the culmination of all the preparatory work you have been doing with ear-training and melodic improvisations. In these exercises, many different kinds of improvisation will be happening at once. The result is often more complicated than the simplicity of the individual parts might indicate. Take your time, and don't be afraid to keep repeating exercises until you feel really ready to go on to the next one.

Round-Robin Ostinati (a game for 4 or more players)

Improvising over an ostinato is a common approach to developing improvisation skills. I first learned a version of this game from Jean-Marc Aeschimann, who taught it as a solfège exercise, but I have since seen many variations on the technique in a variety of improvisational contexts. This one works very well for both singers and instrumentalists.

1. Play or sing the following chord progression in parts, using whatever octave combination is practical for your combination of instruments. Each person chooses one line (soprano, alto, tenor, or bass) and follows it throughout the progression.

EXAMPLE 4.1

cm: i   i   V   i   i   VI V_3^4/V V^7

This is the basic structure on which you will build your improvisation. You'll see that each chord is labeled below the staff with the appropriate Roman numeral. It is very important to understand how different harmonies combine to create a phrase, as well as to learn to identify the quality and function of each chord by its sound. Your ear and your improvisational skills will develop much faster if you take a few minutes to analyze each chord progression provided and write out the progression using Roman numerals. (If you need a refresher in harmonic analysis, please refer to appendix A at the end of this book.)

2. Play the progression again. This time, although you should start with the same pitch you began with the first time, you are not restricted to playing only the line you were assigned; you may jump from the tenor note in one bar to the soprano note in the next, etc. (Still only one note per bar, please!) You will probably find you have a smoother line if you move from one note to another in a way that does not involve large skips. On the other hand, as we saw in chapter 3, large skips can sometimes be very effective in a line when used sparingly and in the right places. Practice and critical listening will help you figure out the right balance of smaller and larger melodic intervals in your line.

3. On the third play-through, you may add a few non-harmonic tones if you desire. One of the easiest ways to do this is through passing and neighbor tones. Play the progression again, and add passing or neigh-

bor tones where appropriate. Again, concentrate on making a beautiful line out of your pitches. Think about how these non-harmonic tones contribute to the direction of your line.

You may want to repeat this stage of the exercise several times; a good way to practice is by having only one person adding non-harmonic tones while the others play only chord tones. This helps everyone hear the non-harmonic tones clearly. Once you all feel comfortable with one set of non-harmonic tones, try having two people adding them, each where appropriate in his or her line. You will soon see how quickly these seemingly small elements begin to distort the structure of the progression, like adding too many spices to your cooking! Later, you will have the opportunity to refine your musical palate and figure out how much spice you want and how much is too much. But for now, just experiment and see what the options are.

4. By now, you should have the progression well in your ears. Come up with a rhythmic pattern that you will use as an ostinato. In executing your ostinato, you may use any combination of notes in the chords, but once you establish your pattern, you should remain consistent. Here are some examples of ostinati:

EXAMPLE 4.2

EXAMPLE 4.2 *Continued*

Please remember that ostinati do not have to begin on the downbeat. You may also use rests within the bar to make your pattern more rhythmically interesting. Play through the progression using your ostinati in place of the long, sustained whole notes of the skeletal chord structure.

5. You now have a solid chordal texture, with some rhythmic interest, which will become a background for a melodic improvisation. Choose one person to improvise a melody. You will not be creating this melody entirely from scratch, since you have the chord progression written out in front of you. Just as you did in steps 2 and 3 of this game, use the written-out chord tones as your "target" notes, and fill in the spaces between with passing tones, neighbor tones, arpeggiated chord tones, scale fragments, etc., just as you have previously practiced in earlier exercises. Remember that melodies also benefit from the inclusion of rests, so that phrases can be clearly distinguished from one another.

Have the ostinato players play through the progression once. The melody player will come in on the second time through the progression.

The first play-through of the ostinati alone is a good opportunity for the melody player to internally audiate what some possible fragments of melody might be. What would it sound like to start with the tenor note in the first bar and go to the alto note in the second bar? Would you want to skip directly there, or use a passing tone to connect them? Begin to imagine little pieces of melody, so you have somewhere to start when it is time to come in, but don't get too caught up in predicting every last detail and then struggling to do it exactly that way. If what comes out isn't what you thought it would be, that's perfectly fine. The more you practice, the more you will learn how to audiate successfully and to know where those audiated pitches live on your instrument. As you continue to play these games, your skill and flexibility will increase.

6. Once you have an idea how the game goes, do it in round-robin form: players take turns improvising melodies over the other ostinati. Because this example ends on a V chord, it is very convenient to just start the progression over again on the next downbeat with a new soloist. Ostinati players may choose a new ostinato with each repetition. When

all players have done a melody, end the improvisation by cadencing on the tonic.

VARIATIONS

1. Texture: To separate the melody from the ostinati by texture, sing the melody and play the ostinati, or vice versa.

2. Quick-response: Instead of the melody proceeding in an orderly manner around the group, the player currently playing the melody gets to decide who should take it next. At the end of the current cycle, the melody player should call out the name of the next person to take over.

3. Multiple melodies: If you have enough players to cover the chord progression, you can try having more than one person improvising a melody at once. There are both joys and challenges to this, as you will discover! It will probably be easiest if the two melody instruments work in different ranges: violin and cello or flute and bassoon, for example.

The Whole Is Greater Than the Sum of Its Parts (a game for 4 or more players)

The use of ostinato patterns as accompaniment is quite common in chamber music, as seen in the following excerpt from the Mozart Clarinet Quintet, 2nd movement (Larghetto):

EXAMPLE 4.3. Mozart: Quintet for Clarinet and Strings, K. 581, 2nd mvt. (Larghetto)

EXAMPLE 4.3 *Continued*

Though ostinato patterns provide a convenient way to combine har-mony with some rhythmic interest, chamber music would be very boring if melody and ostinati were the only two elements. The Mozart clarinet quintet, above, contains another important element besides melody and ostinati: a bass line. One of the most important roles of the bass line is to give line and direction to the harmony (which otherwise would be quite static). For this reason, Mozart differentiates it from the inner voices by giving it different rhythms and a different texture. This makes it easy to hear the bass line and distinguish it from the other things that are going on.

Nor can the other voices live by ostinati alone. Changes in rhythm and texture in the upper voices help give direction to the phrase and make for a more interesting accompaniment. For example, take a look at the following excerpt from Dvořák's *American* quartet:

EXAMPLE 4.4. Dvorak: String Quartet in F Major, Op. 96 (*American*), 1st mvt. (Allegro ma non troppo)

EXAMPLE 4.4 *Continued*

In this excerpt you will see hints of several of the techniques we've used so far: the drone, the "snake," rhythmic ostinati, etc. Rather than sticking with one idea at a time, as we have done up until now, Dvořák uses them in various combinations to make the composition more interesting. Using contrasting rhythms and texture is one way to clarify the role each instrument is playing at a particular moment, and to ensure that what needs to get heard is heard. Exploring how to use rhythm and texture will help you create better improvisations, ones which reflect an understanding of how these different roles interact.

The next several games will help you figure out how to let your ostinato patterns evolve into lines that do more than provide a harmonic and rhythmic structure.

1. Play the following chord progression in parts:

EXAMPLE 4.5

Write out the harmonic progression in Roman numerals under the excerpt.

2. Decide on a meter for your improvisation. You may want to start with $\frac{4}{4}$ first, since that is the meter in which the example is written, but once you are familiar with how the game works, you may want to use different meters for variety.

3. For the first round of this game, we will assign "traditional" chamber music roles to each player. In a string quartet, which will be

used as an example, the first violin traditionally carries the melody, the cello usually has the bass line, and the second violin and viola have the inner voices, which tend to be more accompanimental in nature, though no less important. Later, you will change roles.

Let's begin with the bass line. For this exercise, keep the part fairly simple. Using the bass line of the chord progression as your guide, add some simple rhythms to create a real line. This time, do not use just one rhythmic pattern for the whole of the exercise. Though you do not have to vary your rhythm in each bar, do change it a few times during the course of the improvisation to avoid monotony. Stick with simple rhythms to start; whole, half, and quarter notes are all you need at first. You should always include the bass note of the chord, but you may also include one or two of the other pitches if it makes musical sense. Rests are welcome here, too, though you must make sure that pitches critical to the harmony get heard.

EXAMPLE 4.6. Mozart: String Quartet in d minor, K. 173, 3rd mvt. (Menuetto)

The following excerpts show typical bass line writing from the Classical and Romantic periods. These excerpts are taken from string quartets, but the same principles apply to pieces with other instrumentation.

EXAMPLE 4.7. Mozart: String Quartet in d minor, K. 421, 1st mvt. (Allegro)

EXAMPLE 4.8. Mozart: String Quartet in D Major, K. 155, 1st mvt. (Allegro)

EXAMPLE 4.9. Beethoven: String Quartet in c minor, Op. 18, No. 4, 1st mvt. (Allegro ma non tanto)

EXAMPLE 4.10. Beethoven: String Quartet in C Major, Op. 59, No. 3, 2nd mvt. (Andante con moto quasi Allegretto)

EXAMPLE 4.11. Mendelssohn: Four Pieces for String Quartet, Op. 81: Capriccio (Andante con moto)

Like a great melody, a great bass line should generally be singable, though in the bass line you are more likely to encounter changes of octave and other non-linear types of motion. The bass is crucial to communicating the harmony of the phrase, so bass lines are likely to contain important points of harmonic change. There may be one or two pitches that are particularly critical to successfully communicating the harmony, and the bass line can be particularly valuable in doing this. Keep in mind, however, that the bass line should be exactly that: a line, with notes that flow into one another according to some overall musical plan. Bass lines that only use the roots of the underlying chords tend to be disjunct and disjointed. This is why inversions of chords are so valuable: they allow composers or improvisers to choose the harmony they like but also to create a good line in the bass. Remember the trick of introducing non-harmonic tones through passing and neighbor tones; a few of these sprinkled into your basic bass line will add complexity quickly. Again, use the principle of a lot of sugar and a little spice; if the bass line gets too florid, it will be difficult for others to build on top.

Bass lines may also incorporate patterns listed here as inner voice patterns. Some composers, such as Rossini and Alberti, used patterns like these so extensively that their styles are instantly recognizable. Feel free to borrow whatever you like!

Inner voices: You are responsible for making sure that most of the harmony is represented. Using the inner lines of the chord progression as your guide, add rhythmic patterns so that you create real lines. You may choose ostinato patterns, such as constant eighth notes, but you may also choose to use different patterns throughout your improvisation. You do not need to do the same pattern as each other; one person may choose a constant arpeggiated eighth-note motion while the other plays quarter notes on the first and last beats of each bar. Like the bass line, your parts should strike a balance of continuity and variation. Don't change your pattern every bar, but do change it occasionally during the improvisation, perhaps at a particularly significant chord or color change. As you grow more experienced with improvisation, you will begin to sense appropriate moments for change. You will also start to get a sense for how various inner-voice rhythmic patterns work with one another.

Here are some typical inner voice patterns from Classical and Romantic works. The second violin and viola parts are shown.

EXAMPLE 4.12.
Mozart: String
Quartet in B♭
Major, K. 159,
4th mvt. (Allegro
grazioso)

EXAMPLE 4.13. Mozart: String Quartet in B♭ Major, K. 159, 4th mvt. (Allegro grazioso)

EXAMPLE 4.13 *Continued*

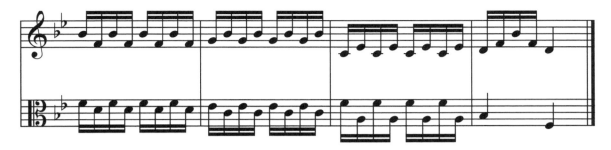

EXAMPLE 4.14. Mozart: String Quartet in G Major, K. 156, 1st. mvt. (Presto)

EXAMPLE 4.15. Mozart: String Quartet in C Major, K. 170, 3rd mvt. (Un poco Adagio)

EXAMPLE 4.16. Mendelssohn: *Four Pieces for String Quartet,* Op. 81: Capriccio (Andante con moto)

EXAMPLE 4.17. Mozart: String Quartet in d minor, K. 421, 4th mvt. (Allegro ma non troppo)

EXAMPLE 4.18. Dvořák: String Quartet in F Major, Op. 96 (*American*), 2nd mvt. (Lento)

EXAMPLE 4.19. Brahms: Quintet for Clarinet and Strings, 4th mvt. (Con moto)

EXAMPLE 4.20. Brahms: Quintet for Clarinet and Strings, 4th mvt. (Con moto)

EXAMPLE 4.21. Brahms: Quintet for Clarinet and Strings, 4th mvt. (Con moto)

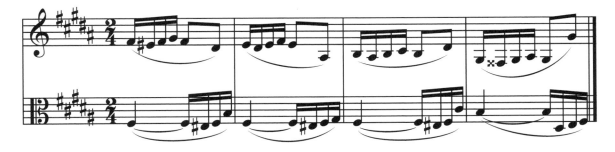

Remember, there are a variety of textures you can choose from. Try some lines using only offbeats or syncopated notes. Use a rhythmic motif. Use special instrumental techniques such as pizzicato. Don't be afraid to use occasional non-harmonic tones; passing tones are particularly easy to work in. And as always, don't forget to use rests!

Melody: Several examples of Classical- and Romantic-era melodies appear in the section on melodic improvisation earlier in this book. Feel free to refer to them whenever you need guidance. The melody you create should ideally be influenced by the texture of the other three parts. You might ask the other players to play their improvisations through once before you enter, so you can hear the qualities of their lines. Since the inner voices and bass line are covering the harmony, you have quite a bit of freedom to be creative with your melody. Use any of the notes in the chord progression as your guideposts. Add non-harmonic tones by using passing or neighbor tones. If you make a "mistake," turn it into an appoggiatura. And one more time, because it's so important: please use rests as well as notes.

A note to all players: Your individual line may seem simple at times, and it is tempting to add complexity to it in all sorts of ways to make it more interesting. Remember that everyone else probably feels the same temptation you do. If you decide to throw in a substantial helping of spicy non-harmonic tones, and everyone else makes the same decision, your addition has in effect been multiplied by four. It is easy to turn an improvisation into disorganized mush by adding too many extra features. As you do more and more of these improvisations, you will gain a sense of how much is too much.

After you have played this game using the melody-harmony roles traditionally assigned to your instrument, do it in round-robin style, with a different person playing the melody at each repetition. Changing the texture of the harmony voices as well will produce stylistically different improvisations.

This game makes a terrific encore for a chamber music recital or concert. You can solicit suggestions from the audience as to key and meter, and improvise a passacaglia on a progression you've picked beforehand. Another effective kind of improvisation for this situation is a kind of theme-and-variations setup, in which each person takes a stylistic element from the previous variation and alters it; the texture should change with each variation. After everyone has had a turn, play the original melody again (as closely as you can remember it). This can be quite impressive when done well.

Get into the habit of thoughtful analysis of what you are playing, both while you are playing it and after you have finished. Did you like the melody you created? Why or why not? Did it sound the way you imagined it would? What parts of it were particularly successful? What parts didn't work as well? How could you change it to make it better, and what does that tell you about how the music works?

A NOTE FOR OTHER ENSEMBLE COMBINATIONS

Woodwind quintets: Bass line, melody, and accompaniment figures found in Classical-era woodwind quintets (such as the works of Reicha and Danzi) are similar to the string excerpts cited above, so the same rules apply. Of course, string players don't have to make explicit allowances for breathing in the way that you do, so their patterns tend to be long and uninterrupted. Create your patterns in the way that works best for you.

Brass quintets: Given the mutable instrumentation of brass quintets and other brass groups throughout the past several centuries, yours is the group with perhaps the least grounding in Classical-era chamber music. Regardless of the paucity of actual brass chamber repertoire from this era, learning to improvise in this harmonic language will benefit you greatly in any circumstance. The kinds of hearing and improvisational skills stressed here will serve you well regardless of whether your current repertoire focuses on music either more ancient or more modern than the Classical-era styles emphasized in this book.

Piano trios and other ensembles with keyboard: Representative Classical- and Romantic-era piano writing can be found in most sonatas and sonatinas from these eras. The patterns are too numerous to list here, and they mix elements of bass line and inner-voice styles. Pianists have the option of playing melody, bass line, and an accompaniment figure or just one or two of those parts. Sometimes the bass line is doubled by the piano, and sometimes each part acts independently. The option is yours.

Means, Motive, and Opportunity (a game for 4 or more players)

One element that makes the different lines of a chamber music piece sound as though they belong together is some rhythmic interaction between the various lines. A common rhythmic motive, repeated in different instrumental or vocal parts, helps unify the rhythmic feel of a piece.

1. Play the following chord progression in parts. Notate the harmonies below the score.

EXAMPLE 4.22

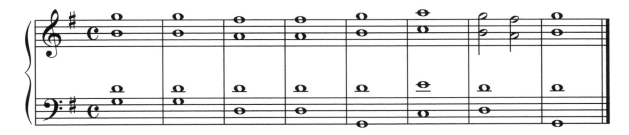

2. Choose a meter for your improvisation. Decide who will experiment with each role: melody, bass line, and harmonic accompaniment.

3. Come up with a short rhythmic motive (two or three beats only, depending on your chosen meter). Here are some sample motives:

EXAMPLE 4.23

4. Play the progression again, with a real melody, bass line, and accompaniment. Each player must use the chosen rhythmic motive at least once in his or her line. It is better to pair the motive with some sort of scalar or arpeggiated motion, rather than playing it on a sustained pitch. The kind of motion used is left up to each individual player; your improvisation will be more interesting if the motive is interpreted differently at different times.

Depending on the length of your motive and your chosen meter, your motive might not have to start on the downbeat of each bar, and it might carry over into the next bar. This gives you a lot of room to be creative and to put the motive where you think it sounds best.

5. Choose a new time signature and a new motive and repeat. Switch roles.

Monkey Hear, Monkey Do (a game for 4 or more players)

Improvising a canon requires excellent hearing and memory skills. Our improvisation will be in the form of a passacaglia, in which one chord progression is repeated over and over. The Canon in D by Pachelbel, one of the world's most famous pieces of music, is an example of this technique. You met this piece earlier when you tried "Music Plus One." The following game is based on a similar, but shorter, chord progression. You could try it with the Pachelbel chord progression if you find this shorter progression too easy.

1. Play the following chord progression in parts. For this game a very slow tempo is best.

EXAMPLE 4.24

Write out the harmonic progression under the staff.

2. Choose two players to play the harmony (Players 3 and 4). Between you, you should represent as many of the notes of the chords as you can, sustained as a soft drone. It will be easier for Players 1 and 2 to hear the melodic line if there is no rhythmic distraction from the accompaniment.

3. The first kind of canon to try is an interrupted canon, also called an echo canon. In this version, Player 1 plays a one-bar melodic fragment, which Player 2 listens to and repeats back to Player 1, while Player 1 is resting. When Player 2 has repeated the fragment, Player 1 creates a new one, and so forth. It is really important to start these melodic fragments simply, with long notes (half notes, quarter notes, etc.). After you have been through a few rounds, slowly start adding smaller note values.

4. After you have mastered the echo canon, try the continuous canon

(see example below). Player 1 will begin the canon by playing a melody (again, start with long notes), and Player 2 will repeat Player 1's melody after one bar *while Player 1 is continuing with a new bar.* Player 2 will need to execute Player 1's first bar while simultaneously listening to the new material. Do at least eight or ten bars, then end the canon at a signal from Player 1. When you are ready, switch roles.

If you get lost, you can always come back in again at the next downbeat, since the harmonic pattern always repeats itself. This game requires a lot of concentration, but it is a great way to make strong aural and kinesthetic connections: you really learn to play what you hear. After some practice at this game, you should also find your skills at written dictation improving.

EXAMPLE OF THE CONTINUOUS CANON   EXAMPLE 4.25

VARIATIONS

1. Interval of repetition: To stretch your memory, allow two bars of Player 1's melody before Player 2 enters.

2. Meter: Use $\frac{12}{8}$ instead of $\frac{4}{4}$. Or, write a new harmonic progression in $\frac{3}{4}$. For an advanced challenge, choose a progression in $\frac{5}{4}$.

3. Canon for three voices: As above, except that Player 3 is now a melody player, entering a bar after Player 2. This is a step up in difficulty for all players, since there is the distraction of an added voice. Note to Player 4: Since you are now the only person playing harmony, do your best to play as many notes of the chord as you can. If multiple pitches are impossible, play the bass line.

Chorale (a game for 4 or more players)

Study the excerpt below:

EXAMPLE 4.26. Schumann: String Quartet in A Major, Op. 41, No. 3, 4th mvt. (Allegro molto vivace)

This excerpt contains only one rhythmic idea, and all parts play this same rhythmic pattern throughout. This kind of completely homophonic texture is not often found in Western instrumental music, since without rhythmic variation a piece can quickly become boring. Schumann uses syncopation, harmonic changes, and a lot of energy from both the tempo and the dotted rhythms to keep this movement interesting, and he alternates homophonic and polyphonic sections within the movement so the listener's attention never wanes.

A more common approach is to balance the chordal appeal of homophonic writing with the textural interest brought by polyphony. The chorales of Bach are considered some of the finest examples of this balance. Bach maintains a fundamentally homophonic chordal texture, with regular harmonic rhythm and a new syllable of text on every chord change, but through the use of different rhythmic values in each of the four parts he also creates melodic lines that interlock contrapuntally in an interesting and beautiful way. The chorales display a wide range of complexity (both rhythmic and harmonic), as shown by the following two examples:

EXAMPLE 4.27. Bach: Chorale No. 59, *Herzliebster Jesu*

EXAMPLE 4.28. Bach: Chorale No. 121, *Werde munter, mein Gemüte*

This homorhythmic technique can be applied to improvisation. It is a good way to experiment with vertical vs. horizontal hearing.

1. Play the following chord progression in parts. Use the existing rhythms.

EXAMPLE 4.29

a.

You will notice that chord changes occur more frequently in this exercise. After all, it is the rare piece of chamber music that is limited to one harmony per measure! This is an example of how harmonic rhythm (the various lengths of time that each harmony is heard, and the rate at which the harmonies change) can impact our sense of direction and energy in a phrase.

Write out the harmonic progression under the score.

2. As a group, develop a simple rhythmic motive that you'll repeat as an ostinato, as in the Schumann excerpt above. For your first try, limit yourselves to half notes, quarter notes, and eighth notes. Later you can add more complicated rhythms.

3. Play through the above progression using your simple rhythmic pattern, but be sure to make the harmonic changes according to the harmonic rhythm provided in the written exercise. This might mean that you change harmony within your ostinato pattern. So you are keeping track of two rhythmic ideas at once: the rhythms of your ostinato on the micro-level, and the harmonic rhythm of the chord changes in the progression on the larger level.

The first time through, limit yourselves to chord tones only (no non-harmonic tones). After you have that under your belt, add non-harmonic tones in the form of passing tones, neighbor tones, chromaticism, and appoggiaturas. You will see that even though each person may feel that he or she is only adding a moderate number of non-harmonic tones, when these additions are multiplied by four the effect can be huge.

4. After you've mastered the ostinato and the use of non-harmonic tones, create a more complicated rhythmic motif. You might use syncopation, hemiolas, or rests to make it more challenging. Play the progression again with your revised pattern. If you like, play the progression a third time with two players playing the first pattern and the others playing the second one. See how well the two patterns go together.

5. Repeat this procedure with the more complicated chord progression printed below. Note the differences you feel because of the more varied harmonic rhythm of this progression.

EXAMPLE 4.30

Musical Volleyball (a game for 4 or more players)

There are many possible levels of musical structure. Motives may be linked up to form phrases, and phrases may be combined to form periods or other larger groupings. For example, take a look at the following excerpt from a Mozart string quartet:

EXAMPLE 4.31.
Mozart: String
Quartet in D
Major, K. 575,
2nd mvt.
(Andante)

In this example, each player gets one statement of a phrase, but the phrases combine to form a larger unit. If you do a harmonic analysis of Mozart's work, you will see that the first phrase ends with a half cadence, the second phrase ends with a full cadence, the third phrase ends with a half cadence in from a related key, and the fourth phrase cadences fully in that new key. It is the combination of these individual phrases, shared by all the players, that creates the larger unit. In this example, all four phrases share the same rhythm and the same basic motif (though there are slight variations from one to the next).

We can apply this technique to improvisation on a smaller scale with the following exercise, which is not as complicated as the instructions might lead you to believe. Your ear will tell you how the game works.

EXAMPLE 4.32   1. Play the following chord progression in parts:

Write out the harmonic symbols beneath the notes.

2. Choose a meter for your improvisation, and start thinking of accompaniment patterns. For your first go at this game, choose simple ostinato accompaniments so you can really concentrate on the melody. Later, you can spice up the accompaniment patterns a bit if you like. Notice, however, the simplicity of the accompaniment in the Mozart example—sometimes less really is more.

3. Play through the progression again using your ostinato patterns.

4. Each of you will play a portion of the melody, so decide among yourselves the order of players. Player 1 is responsible for coming up with a two-bar phraselet that the other players will imitate when their turn comes for the melody. Make it simple so that the other players can easily adapt it when their turns come around.

As a jumping-off point, you might decide to tell everyone in advance that the phraselet to be copied will begin on the note that is the root of the chord. This means that the other players can look ahead in the music and see what notes they'll be starting on for their adaptations, which eliminates some of the anxiety that frequently surrounds this game. As you become more expert in improvisation, you won't need to specify the starting pitch.

5. Play through the progression again, at a slow tempo, with Player 1 improvising his or her melodic motive in the first two bars while the others play ostinati. In bar 3, Player 1 plays his or her ostinato while Player 2 takes over the melody, playing the same motive Player 1 played, but adapted to the harmony of bars 3 and 4. Player 3 takes the melody for bars 5 and 6, and Player 4 for bars 7 and 8.

6. Change the order of players so that everyone gets the chance to come up with an original phraselet.

EXAMPLE 4.33

Switch and Signal (a game for 4 or more players)

This is a quick-response game involving the use of a musical signal.

EXAMPLE 4.34

1. Play the following progression in parts:

Write out the harmonic progression in Roman numerals under the score.

2. Choose an order of players to create the melody. This order will repeat so that after Player 4 is finished, Player 1 will begin again. Also choose a meter for your improvisation, and begin thinking of ostinato patterns. As in the Musical Volleyball game, ostinati are recommended for your first experience with this exercise. As you gain experience in juggling more than one musical idea at a time (increasing your capacity for divided attention), you'll be able to create more complicated accompaniments.

3. The game works as follows: Player 1 will begin improvising a melody while the others play ostinati accompaniments (you will find that a slow tempo is best for this game until you really get the hang of it) Somewhere in the melody Player 1 will insert a musical signal, which all of you together will agree on beforehand. When the signal is played, the melody goes to Player 2 on the next beat, while Player 1 reverts to an ostinato. Player 2 does not have to play the same melody as Player 1, although keeping some elements will ensure some degree of musical continuity. When Player 2 plays the signal, Player 3 takes the melody on the next beat, and so on.

The musical signal can be anything that you agree on as a group, and it could occur anywhere within the bar or phrase. In the beginning, don't make the signal too short, or the person who is about to take the melody may not have enough time to react. For example, your starting signal could be two sixteenth notes and a quarter on a repeated pitch (as in the example below), or four sixteenth notes and a quarter which spell out an arpeggio.

Take a look at an example of how this might work. The accompaniment parts are represented with block chords only for the sake of clarity. For this example, the signal is:

EXAMPLE 4.35

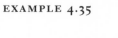

EXAMPLE 4.36

In this example, the signal happens at the same place in the first two phrases, but later on it gets used at other places within the phrase. Also, since the actual pitches being played at any given time will vary depending on the chord, it's best to define your signal by describing it (three notes on the same pitch) rather than by pinning it down to a specific note name ("three repeated Gs").

VARIATIONS

Your signal could indicate something other than switching melody players. It could mean to switch the tonality from major to minor, to transpose the music up or down a whole step, or for everyone to substitute rests for the next four beats' worth of music. It could mean to play twice as fast, or twice as slow. This is one of the most versatile games in the book; any variation you can imagine is possible.

When you are real pros at using a single signal (and only when you are real pros), add another signal with another condition. Your first signal might indicate to change melody player, the second to change to the minor mode, etc. These signals can operate independently of each other.

These are advanced variations; performing them with ease requires true mastery of ear, brain, and hands, but they are worth practicing and working on.

Dialogue (Melody/Countermelody Echo) (a game for 4 or more players)

EXAMPLE 4.37   Play the following progression in parts:

Identify the harmonic progression and write it out under the example. What compositional technique does this example contain? This technique will be very useful to us in this improvisation.

This is a game using melody and countermelody. In this exercise, we will have melody and countermelody in echo form rather than occurring simultaneously. Choose two players to play melody and two to play accompaniment; as an example, we will use a string quartet in which we begin with first violin and viola as melody instruments and second violin and cello as accompaniment. Note: This puts the whole burden of harmonic representation on only two accompanimental voices; make sure you improvise lines that produce a fairly complete presentation of the underlying chords. If you have more than four players in your ensemble, this burden is not quite so heavy.

1. Play the progression with the two accompanimental voices only, using whatever meter, textures, and rhythmic patterns you like.

2. Play the progression again, adding the two melody instruments as follows: During the first bar, the first violin should improvise a one-bar melody, while the viola rests. During the second bar, the violin is silent and the viola improvises a countermelody. In the third bar, the violin takes over again, playing the same melody he or she used during the first bar but adapting it to the change in harmony. The two melody instru-

ments alternate measures until the last two bars are reached. For the last two bars, both instruments simultaneously improvise something which brings their individual phrases to a satisfactory cadence.

A note on the countermelody: This is not an exercise in imitation, so the countermelody should not seek to duplicate the melody. Instead, create something original but complementary. For example, if the melody involves scalar motion going up, you might create a countermelody using arpeggiated motion going down, or many shorter note values where the original used long notes. The two ideas can be quite distinct in texture. Repeat, changing roles.

An example of a possible combination appears below: EXAMPLE 4.38

Pas de Deux (a game for 4 or more players)

EXAMPLE 4.39.
Verdi: Prelude
from *La Traviata*

In the previous game, you experimented with alternating melody and countermelody, each taking its turn in alternate bars. But melody and countermelody can also occur simultaneously. Below is an example from the prelude to Verdi's opera *La Traviata*:

EXAMPLE 4.39 *Continued*

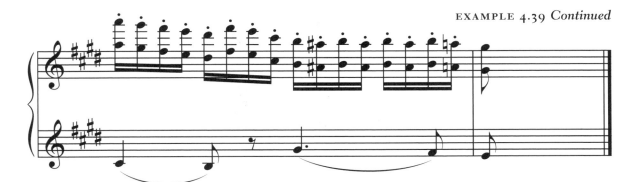

There are a number of reasons that this is a successful juxtaposition of melody and countermelody:

· The two melodies have very different textures
· They are widely separated in register
· They are quite different rhythmically (one uses long, sustained notes; the other, short notes separated by rests)
· The melodic lines move in opposite directions.

In addition, although the excerpt above does not show it, the melody in the lower part was heard once through by itself before the upper voice entered. Therefore, the audience was already familiar with it and did not have to simultaneously process both it and the upper voice as new tunes. Introducing one tune by itself first before pairing it with the other is a good technique for working with melodies and countermelodies.

Keep these characteristics in mind as you do the following exercise. Though they are not hard-and-fast rules, they are good guidelines that will help you create successful melody/countermelody combinations.

1. Play the following chord progression in parts: EXAMPLE 4.40

Write out the harmonic progression beneath the staff.

2. Choose one person to play the melody and one to play the countermelody. The other two players are responsible for the harmony. If you wish to change the meter or harmonic rhythm from what is printed above, feel free to do so.

3. The harmony players may wish to decide ahead of time on a par-

ticular texture to use for their accompaniment. After this decision is
made, harmony players should play through the progression, using whatever accompaniment patterns they choose.

4. Without pause, repeat the phrase, adding the melody player only.
The improvised melody should fit the style of the accompaniment (this
will allow the countermelody to create all the contrast). Keep the melody
simple! There are two reasons for this: (a) you will need to remember the
melody fairly precisely in order to play it again, and (b) the real beauty
of the complete improvisation is in the interaction of the melody and
countermelody, so it is best not to make either line too florid at first.

5. Without pause, repeat the phrase again. This time the melody
player is silent and the countermelody player creates an improvisation in
a contrasting style. Like the melody, the countermelody should not be
too complicated at first. Later, you can experiment with juxtaposing two
lines that are much more ornate, or combining a complex line with a
simple one.

6. Without pause, repeat the phrase again, this time with all parts.
This is the test of how well your melody and countermelody work together, as well as the test of how well the melody and countermelody
players are able to remember their lines!

One important difference between the echo and simultaneous meth-
ods of melody/countermelody improvisation is the manner in which the
phrase develops. In the echo version, both melody and countermelody
are quite short, and since they occur in alternating bars neither one alone
really fills out a phrase. The balance of the phrase depends on the presence of both parts. In the simultaneous method, however, both melody
and countermelody are self-sufficient, complete phrases with their own
direction and line, and the two weave in and out of each other without
endangering the harmonic support of the whole.

Pedal to the Metal (a game for 4 or more players)

One of the most powerful compositional techniques for supporting the
direction and tension of a phrase is the pedal. Although it is most commonly used in the bass line, it can occur in any voice. In this exercise, you
will each get the opportunity to explore the impact of a pedal tone on a
phrase.

1. Play the following progression in parts. Notate the harmony below
the staff.

EXAMPLE 4.41

2. Choose a meter and tempo for your progression. The lowest-sounding instrument in your group should play the bass line; the others may divide up melody and harmony as you like.

3. Look carefully at the progression and locate where a pedal tone could be sustained. In order to be a true pedal, one voice must maintain the same pitch while the harmonies change around it. Try to find at least three consecutive harmonies which contain a common tone. These are the places where a pedal will be most successful.

4. In the above example, the pedal is in the bass line. Play through the improvisation with a created melody and inner voices. For the first time through, play the bass line as long notes. When you reach the pedal, sustain it through continuously, changing bow or taking a new breath as infrequently as possible. This should help you feel the pedal tone's ability to build and sustain tension toward an arrival point.

5. Play through the example again with a regular bass line. You may choose whether to play a sustained note for the pedal bars or to substitute some other rhythmic pattern. Try to really use the pedal to heighten the energy and tension within the progression.

In this progression, the pedal lasts only a few bars, but in a composed piece it may last much longer. The power of the pedal is in its ability to sustain a ground pitch against rising tension in other voices. For this reason, the color of the pitch changes depending on the harmony that fits around it. Sometimes the pedal is actually a non-chord tone of one or more of the sonorities passing over it. The pedal serves to drive the tension toward its eventual resolution, and makes that resolution more satisfying when it is reached. In general, the tensile quality of a pedal grows as it approaches the point of ultimate tension and release. It is more intense when the chords over it are dissonant, and more relaxed when they are consonant. These effects are achieved through the following factors, alone or in combination: crescendo, tone color, intensity of sound, and use of vibrato.

6. Play the progression again. When you reach the pedal notes, do not play the sustained pedal tone. Choose other notes in the harmony to play. Then play the progression again, with the pedal back in. You should hear a definite difference in the quality of direction of the phrase.

7. Play the progression through several more times, changing roles so that everyone gets a chance to play the pedal.

Does register influence the effectiveness of the pedal tone? Compare the effect of a performance in which the bass had the pedal with one in which the pedal appeared in a higher register. Do they produce the same effect? What did you like about each version?

Son of Sing and Play (a game for 4 or more players)

Yes, it's your old friend Sing and Play, back in ensemble form.

1. Play through the following chord progression in parts. Write out the harmony below the staff.

EXAMPLE 4.42

2. Decide who will play melody, bass line, and harmony. If you like, change the meter or harmonic rhythm.
3. Choose a musical signal, as in the Switch and Signal game. The melody and bass line players are the only two allowed to use the signal.
4. Begin improvising. Go through the complete progression at least once, repeating when you get to the end. Beginning with the second repetition, when you hear the melody player give the signal, switch from playing your part to singing it.
5. When the bass line player sings the signal, go back to playing. Repeat.
6. End your improvisation by resolving to the tonic. Repeat, switching roles.

Freeze Frame (a game for 4 or more players)

This is a souped-up version of the Pitch Switch game you played at the very beginning of this book.

Play the following chord progression in parts.

EXAMPLE 4.43

Choose two people to be leaders. Play the chord progression again, slowly. At any time, Leader 1 may call "Freeze!"—which means you should continue to hold out whatever pitch you're on as if it had a fermata. Close your eyes and listen to the other notes being played. After a moment, Leader 2 should call "Change!"—at which point you are each to change to the pitch of the person on your right. Hold the chord for a minute to verify that it's correct, then open your eyes to find the note you are playing in the chord. When Leader 1 calls "Go!" continue playing the progression from your new place in the hierarchy of the chord. Keep repeating the progression until you have made several switches. On Leader 1's signal, finish the last play-through with a cadence on the tonic.

This game can also be done with any of the other chord progressions in this book. And you may combine it with "Son of Sing and Play" so that various verbal signals tell you either to switch from singing to playing or to change parts with other players.

Dummy Up (a game for 4 or more players)

If you have ever played bridge, you are probably familiar with the idea of a "dummy"—one person sits out while the other three play out the hand. Here, the concept is applied to a quick-response improvisational game.

Play the following chord progression in parts:

EXAMPLE 4.44

Write out the harmonic progression below the staff.

Your realization of this progression will have only three parts: melody, bass line, and harmony. This means that at any given moment, three of you will be playing and one of you will be sitting out (as the "dummy").

1. Choose three players, one each for melody, bass line, and harmony. Pick a meter and a tempo; a slow tempo is suggested for your first try.

2. Players 1, 2, and 3 begin improvising. Play through the whole progression at least once so you become more familiar with the harmonies. Starting with the second repetition, any player may drop out at the start of any measure. When this happens, the player who has been "dummy" must jump in and fill the vacant role. The player who has just dropped out immediately becomes dummy and must jump in when the next opening occurs.

It is vital for all players to actively listen at all times so that the transitions between players will be as seamless as possible. When jumping in to take over the melody, try to keep the same style as the person before you; you may change styles and textures at the repeat of the phrase. The same applies to the bass line and accompaniment roles. If you change players often enough, you will each get a chance to play all three roles.

One of the most challenging aspects of this game is how to manage the transition between players. If you are planning to drop out, you must communicate your intention to the dummy player so that he or she can prepare to jump in. Without communication, the improvisation will collapse. Eye contact, body movement, and cueing are all excellent ways to let the dummy player know that he or she must jump in at the next bar line. Also, since only one person can drop out at a time, all four players are responsible for maintaining an awareness of who's about to drop out, who's about to come in, and what role each person is playing.

If you have difficulty managing the transition through eye contact and body language, try adding a musical signal, like that you used in the Switch and Signal game. Eliminate the signal when you are more confident.

VARIATION

In this variant, whoever is "dummy" has control over the change in players. You will need a lot of space, so spread your group out much more than you usually do. Three players begin playing as above. When the dummy player wants to jump in, he or she stands behind the person whose part he or she will take over and taps that person on the shoulder. Immediately that person gets up and the dummy player sits down in his or her place. The new dummy chooses someone else's place to take. In this version, musical roles are set by physical position: whoever is sitting in chair A will always have the melody, chair B will always have accompaniment, and chair C will always have the bass line.

Bartók Had a Little Lamb (a game for 4 or more players)

In the previous improvisations, we have concentrated on establishing a harmonic progression and then constructing a melody to fit. But we could also start with a melody and then find different ways in which it could be harmonized.

Study the following excerpt. The orchestration has been reduced.

EXAMPLE 4.45. Bartók: Concerto for Orchestra, 4th mvt. (Intermezzo Interrotto) (Allegretto)

Bartók takes the same melodic snippet and harmonizes it in several different ways. Play through the excerpt so you hear the different sound of each rendition.

In homage to Bartók, we also will take a simple tune and experiment with different ways of harmonizing it. I first learned this technique from the Oberlin Conservatory of Music's Professor Herb Henke, who was one of my piano improvisation teachers during summers spent at the Carnegie Mellon University Summer Dalcroze Institute. He suggested that we each take a well-known melody and harmonize it in a non-traditional way. Herb's favorite was "Twinkle, Twinkle, Little Star," but we will be using a different children's tune here.

Unlike most of the other games in this book, this will require a little advance preparation. If you do this as a solo improvisation at the piano, you have simultaneous control over all the voices, so you can make up chord changes on the fly. If this is done as an ensemble exercise, however, more structure is needed. This gives everyone a chance to try their hand at a little composition.

Each person in the group should write out the melody line in an agreed-upon key. It is provided below in the key of C Major:

EXAMPLE 4.46

The traditional harmonization of this tune relies on just a few harmonies. Write them out with Roman numerals beneath the melody.

Now it's time to experiment with some unusual harmonizations. Let's assume we do want to start with a I chord on the first note. But the second note might start to take us away from C Major into a different key, depending on what kind of chord we use to harmonize it. Here is a sample of a possible non-traditional harmonization of this melody:

EXAMPLE 4.47

Each person should prepare a version of the piece using whatever harmonies he or she finds appealing. You can be as conservative or as outlandish as you desire, since the goal is to create a rendition with interesting colors, not necessarily one that adheres to traditional harmonic guidelines. In addition to chordal harmonies, you might want to experiment with quartal or quintal harmonies, pentatonic scales, etc.

Play through all the versions. What did you like or dislike about each?

5   From Sight to Sound: Getting off the Page

The next goal is getting off the page—improvising without using the written-out realizations provided. You may have found yourselves starting this process automatically, relying less on your eyes and more on your ears as your skills have grown. If not, now is the time to leave the nest and fly free of the printed page. This step is like taking the training wheels off a bicycle—you may garner a couple of skinned knees and scraped elbows your first few times out, but once you get your balance you will be able to go much farther, and with greater ease than before.

Navigating through an unfamiliar environment is not always easy. Until you have had experience with all the different kinds of chords, it can be very difficult to tell the difference between them. At the start, you may not even be able to tell the difference between a I chord and a V chord, let alone identify the subtle shadings of various predominants. But the more you immerse yourself in listening to all kinds of sonorities, the more individual sounds will begin to emerge from the fog. You will begin to recognize these patterns of related sounds and have an idea of how they might be grouped together. Remember that in Western harmony, chords are defined by their functions: tonic, dominant, predominant, etc. The easiest chord progression to pick up is from dominant to tonic (V–I). Once you have this in your ear, you will start to notice that chords immediately preceding the dominant have certain recognizable sounds, or that the V–I relationship often includes a cadential dominant instead of an ordinary V chord, etc.

Until now, you have approached each improvisation by playing a chord progression that has been realized for you. Because several of these exercises deal with how sonorities go together to create a phrase, you will need to be able to associate the sonority of a chord with its Roman numeral. Too much reliance on the written-out chords will only hinder you here, because in some exercises you will need to substitute one chord for another, or to create your own progression on the spot. This is why you were encouraged to write a Roman numeral analysis of each progression as you went along. Each time you analyze something that you play, it strengthens the association between symbol and sonority.

The shift toward greater reliance on the ear can be daunting, so approach it gradually. After all, you are learning to hear things in a new way, and that always takes time. The first few games in this section will stretch your abilities a little at a time. Take as long as you need with these exercises; don't go on until you feel ready. If you consistently have trouble with some of the more advanced exercises, come back to the earlier ones for a while, then try the harder ones again. Don't be discouraged—this ability will not come overnight, but it will come.

Wait Your Ternary (a game for 4 or more players)

The minuet/trio often found in symphonies and chamber music is an example of what's called a ternary (three-part) or ABA form. The first section, called A, establishes the key and mood of the movement. The middle section, the B section, is a contrasting section which will have a new melody and which is often in a different key. The piece ends with a repeat of the A section.

In this game, you will create a miniature piece in ternary form using only three phrases: an A phrase, a B phrase, and a repeat of the A phrase.

1. Play through the following chord progressions in parts. Analyze the harmony below the staff. What is the relation between these two keys?

EXAMPLE 5.1

EXAMPLE 5.2

2. Decide who will play melody, who will play the bass line, and who will be the inner voices. These roles should remain the same for both A sections, but you may want to change roles for the B section.

3. Improvise your way through the A section. Without stopping, go directly into the B section. After the B section, play the A section again, trying to repeat your first improvisation as closely as possible. It does not need to be exactly the same (though that would be nice, and a good way to train your aural memory), but it does need to be close enough to be recognizable as the original A section material. This will help train your brain and ears to remember and recreate what you hear.

One thing that often happens in minuet/trio movements in symphonies is that during the trio the melody goes to a different instrument or group of instruments. This is a good variation for your improvisation.

Home Away from Home (a game for 4 or more players)

The progressions you have worked on thus far have not modulated. They have begun and ended in the same key. But staying in the same key all the time would quickly become boring. This game is a preparatory study for improvising a set of modulating phrases, and it will help you reduce your dependency on the printed page as an improvisational crutch.

Play through the following progression in parts. Notate the harmonic progression beneath the staff:

EXAMPLE 5.3

Play the progression in parts several times, concentrating on two things: the notes of the individual line you are playing, and the overall sonorities of the chords. Now play it through again with your eyes closed. If anything sounds different than it did with your eyes open, stop and play it through again. Try to memorize the sequence of sonorities and how your line weaves in and out of them.

This phrase also does not modulate. But we can create the effect of modulation by transposing the phrase to a different key. Here is where your memory of your line and the sequence of sonorities is essential, because you must duplicate them in a different key.

When you can play the original phrase in all parts with your eyes closed, transpose it to the key of G. If transposition is not something you do as part of your daily activities, you may wish to write it out first (I've provided it here as a way for you to check your transposition).

EXAMPLE 5.4

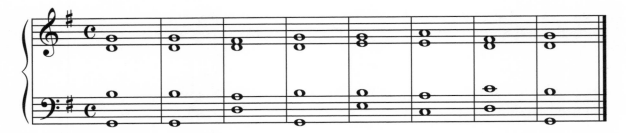

Don't let this become a habit, though; the goal is to develop your ear so that you don't need to write it out. Remember that your line will be made up of the same series of intervals as it was in the original key, although your starting pitch will be different and you may need to change octaves midstream depending on the range of your instrument. If you hear that any of the chords are a different sonority than they were in the original key, stop and check your notes very carefully.

When you have mastered the progression in the keys of C and G, play it in the key of F. This time, don't even be tempted to write out the notes. Use only your ears.

You have now played the same progression in the keys of C, F, and G. In C major, these represent the keys of I, IV, and V, respectively. You could reasonably expect modulation to one or more of these keys in a piece written in C major. So, you can use these three keys to create a little piece. If this kind of pattern were actually to occur in a piece of music, the different keys would be connected by modulating sections so that the transitions would not be as abrupt as they are here. But what we are practicing here is just the skill of remembering a series of harmonies and transposing them by ear to different keys. In the next game we will work on modulating transitions.

1. Play the progression through in the key of C.
2. Without pause, play it again in the key of G.
3. Without pause, play it again in the key of F.
4. Without pause, play it again in the original key.

Repeat this sequence until you are comfortable with the basic progression in all the keys. On your next play-through, add a melody. Begin to add rhythmic accompanimental patterns. When you are fluent with the basic progression, change roles at each repetition so that a different player plays the melody in each key. You may keep the same melody (good test of memory, but not such an interesting improvisation) or vary it with each change in tonality (not as easy, but a more interesting result).

This is an advanced game that requires excellent hearing skills, so don't be disappointed if your first try is not successful or if your group has difficulty. Work on some of the other games and keep coming back to this one; you will do better every time.

You Can't Get There from Here (a game for 4 or more players)

This modulation game will challenge your command of harmony and your quick-thinking skills.

1. Play the following piece of a chord progression in parts as usual. Identify the key and harmonic progression.

EXAMPLE 5.5

2. Now play it with the second half of the progression (bars 5–8). How does the second half relate to the first half?

EXAMPLE 5.6

This is a modulating phrase that arrives at a new key via a secondary dominant. In the above example, we go from the key of C major (I) to the key of G major (V) via the secondary dominant of G (V/V), which is in bar 6 of the excerpt.

3. Play all eight bars of the progression through again. If you'd like, you can change the meter or harmonic rhythm and add a melody and ostinato patterns. Realize the other voices (bass line and harmony) when you are ready.

4. Play it again, but start in C minor rather than C major (since you are modulating to the key of the dominant, which is generally major whether the home tonality is major or minor, your arrival in G will remain in the major mode).

5. This is where it gets tricky. Play the progression again, but change

the destination key. Instead of modulating to V, modulate to vi. You can do this by substituting a V/vi for the V/V, then keeping all the other chord relationships consistent in the new key. (This is written out below.) Again, start with playing the progression in parts, then melody with ostinati, then realized parts.

EXAMPLE 5.7

Experiment with as many different harmonic destinations as you can. The crucial task is figuring out what notes are in the secondary dominant chord. If you need help, arrange the voicing so that the secondary dominant chord is always played in root position. This way, everyone can hear the root of the chord in the lowest-pitched instrument in your group and it will be easier to arpeggiate correctly. Once you have the right secondary dominant, rely on your ears to guide you through the rest of the progression. Here are some possible destinations:

For major progressions: modulate to the key of V, vi, IV, ii
For minor progressions: modulate to the key of V, III, VI, iv
Feel free to add your own favorites to the above list.

Circular Reasoning (a game for 4 or more players)

This is a continuation of the previous modulating game, with a new twist. In order to create the sense of a real modulation, the new key must be firmly established. You will do this by alternating a series of modulating and non-modulating phrases.

1. Play the following progression in parts and analyze the harmonies. Call this Progression A.

EXAMPLE 5.8

2. Play the following progression in parts and analyze the harmonies. This is Progression B, taken from the previous game, with some small alterations.

EXAMPLE 5.9

3. Choose a meter and a tempo for your improvisation, and decide an order in which each person will play melody, harmony, and bass line. Play through Progression A, followed without pause by Progression B.

4. When you reach the end of Progression B and have modulated to a new key, play Progression A again, *in the new key*. You will need to rely on your ears and your Roman numeral notation for this, not on the written-out realization in the old key. When you've mastered this, you may also change roles at this point so that a new person is playing the melody in the new key.

5. This should be immediately followed by Progression B, beginning in the new key, which through modulation will take you to a third key. Again, switch roles. Keep alternating Progressions A and B as you move through the circle of fifths.

Keep the bass line very simple; this will be extremely helpful for those who are building harmonies on top. You may also wish to simplify the game by not changing roles at every repeat of Progression A. As you become more accomplished, introduce changes of texture with each new key. Also, experiment with changing the quality of your melodic material: your line for Progression A can be true melody, but your line for Progression B could be intended more to set up the next person's melody than to be overly juicy itself. Your material for Progression B may be more episodic in nature.

When you have explored all the aspects of the circle of fifths, use a different interval for modulating. Just as in the previous game, this is achieved very simply by changing the secondary dominant in Progression B. Changing the V/V to a V/IV, for example, will mean that you travel around the circle of fifths in the opposite direction. Modulation by a third is also a common compositional device, particularly when going from one key to its relative minor or major.

Name That Tune (a game for 4 or more players)

This simple game is a means of assessing your ability to identify harmonies by ear.

1. Players 1, 2, and 3 will together choose a harmonic progression from earlier in the book. They will tell Player 4 the key of the progression and will play a tonic chord.
2. Players 1, 2, and 3 will play the progression once through, slowly, while Player 4 listens. When they play it the second time, Player 4 must identify each chord by its Roman numeral.

There are many different ways to go about learning to take harmonic dictation (which is essentially what this game is all about). Some rely more on your ear, some more on your brain and common sense (though ideally both faculties are always involved). If you have a different method from the suggestions given here, then by all means, use it.

One way to identify chords is by hearing their overall colors, and one of the most important keys to developing this ability is knowing the crucial notes which determine harmony. For example, differentiating between ii and IV is sometimes surprisingly difficult, even though one is clearly major and the other minor. In addition to really hearing the major/minor distinction, hearing the presence of scale degree 2 in the mix will tell you it must be a ii chord. Also, each chord in a progression has a certain color, and learning to distinguish these colors will also help you identify the chords. Not only are chords major or minor, they are also consonant or dissonant, bright or dull. For a refresher on the qualities of diatonic chords in major and minor keys, see appendix A at the back of the book.

If you are having difficulty distinguishing between the subtleties of certain chords, start by identifying three main categories: tonic, dominant, and "everything else." From there, begin to search out the distinguishing colors of the predominant chords (ii, IV, V/V, vi, etc.), which will fall into the "everything else" category. Once you have those straight, tackle the other diatonic chords within a key. For example, iii has a color all its own—it's not a tonic, it's not a dominant, and it's not a predominant. If you hear chromaticism, you might have a secondary dominant or some other kind of borrowed chord. Remember that since Roman numeral analysis is based on function, you may not be able to correctly identify a chord until you hear its resolution. If you have a secondary dominant, though, you can probably sense what its chord of resolution will be.

You should also learn to identify the sound of common cadential formulas. The four most frequent in the classical style are the authentic (V–I), half (ending on V), deceptive (V–vi), and plagal (IV–I) cadences.

Another way to approach this task is to identify the root of each chord and use logic (with aural confirmation) to figure out the rest. If this is difficult for you, go back to the "Getting to the Root of the Problem" game in chapter 2 and practice. If you know the root of a chord, you can figure out the other notes and identify the harmonic role of the chord. This is helpful when you are having trouble distinguishing between two chords with several notes in common. Remember, the root is not always the lowest-sounding pitch. A IV and a ii⁶ chord both have the same pitch in the bass, but they have different roots.

Being Diana Ross (a game for 4 or more players)

Play through the following progressions. Progression 1 is easier than Progression 2. For both progressions, notate the harmony below the staff:

EXAMPLE 5.10

EXAMPLE 5.11

In a four-player game, one person will play melody, one will play bass line, and the other two will cover the harmony.

1. Play the progression through several times without the melody. The melody player should be listening carefully, trying to memorize the sonorities. While you are listening, try to imagine a possible melody that fits the progression.

2. Add the melody. Everyone except the melody player should play from the score (these are the Supremes), but the melody player must

play *only by ear*, without looking at the page. (Congratulations! You're Diana Ross.)

3. Change melody players and repeat the exercise. Change the texture of the accompaniment as well.

Since the non-melody players are playing from the score, they are responsible for checking that the melody player includes the right notes.

Don't be afraid to make a mistake when improvising your melodies. If you land on a non-chord tone, turn it into an appoggiatura. Resolve it through chromaticism. The only way you will really train your ear is by making mistakes, then figuring out how to fix them. Also, the more you can plan ahead, the better off you will be. For example, if you know a ii chord is coming up, try to arrange your line so you can include scale degree 2 somewhere in that bar. And on top of everything else, keep a steady pulse at all times!

Dinner at a Chinese Restaurant (a game for 4 or more players)

A popular feature of many Chinese restaurants is the family dinner special, in which you get a certain number of dishes from those listed in Column A on the menu and a certain number from Column B. Here, that concept is used to create a foundation for improvisation.

1. Choose two patterns from Column A and two patterns from Column B. Use either major or minor mode, but not both.

EXAMPLE 5.12

Column A   *Column B*

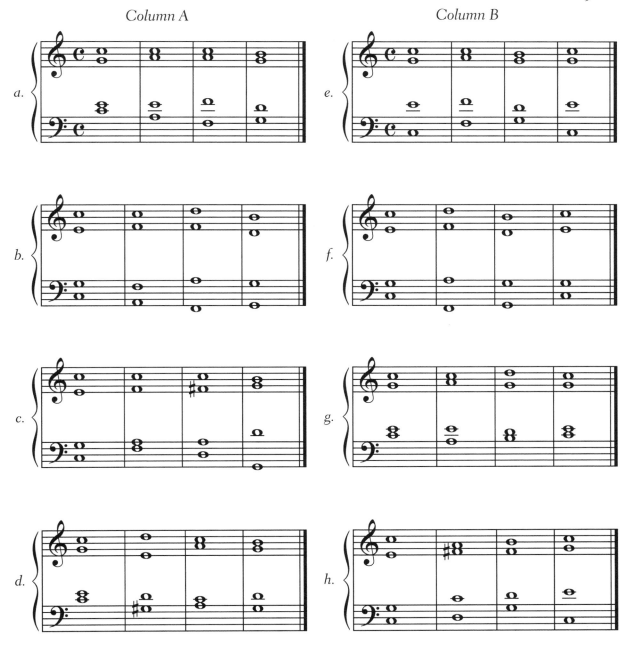

EXAMPLE 5.13

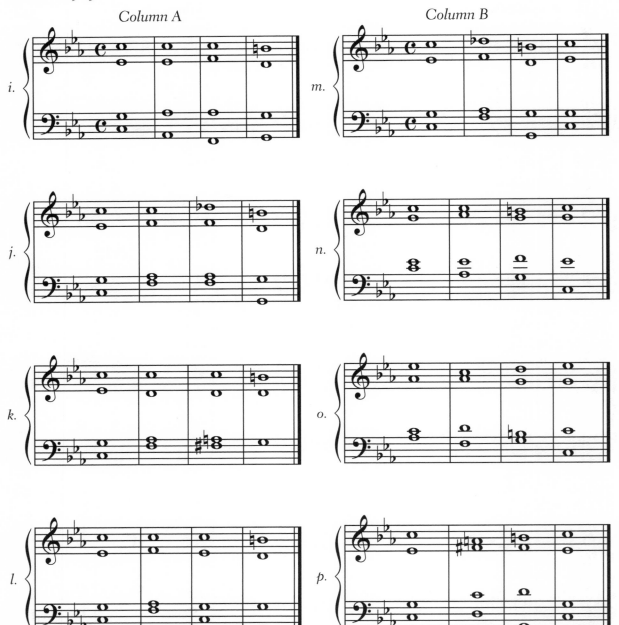

2. Decide on an order for your four patterns. You should alternate between the two columns, beginning with Column A. Also decide on a key and a meter.

3. Assign each person one of the progressions you have chosen. If you have fewer than four players, one person will have to go twice; if more than four, one person will have to sit out this round. You will each be responsible for improvising a melody for the pattern you are assigned.

4. Play through the progressions once with all players using ostinato patterns only. Since you are doing this without writing out the pitches, using ostinati will allow you to concentrate on playing the right harmonies. There should be no break between the four patterns.

5. When everyone is comfortable with the harmony, play it through again, adding melodies above the ostinati.

It's So Nice, You Can Do It Twice (a game for 4 or more players)

Another great thing about Chinese food is that there are always leftovers. Too much food on your plate can be overwhelming; you know you just can't digest all of it in one sitting. The same is true with improvisation: trying to do too many new things at the same time is frustrating. So this game is really just some musical leftovers: a continuation of the last game, freshened up by an added twist or two.

1. Choose two patterns from Column A and two patterns from Column B.

EXAMPLE 5.14

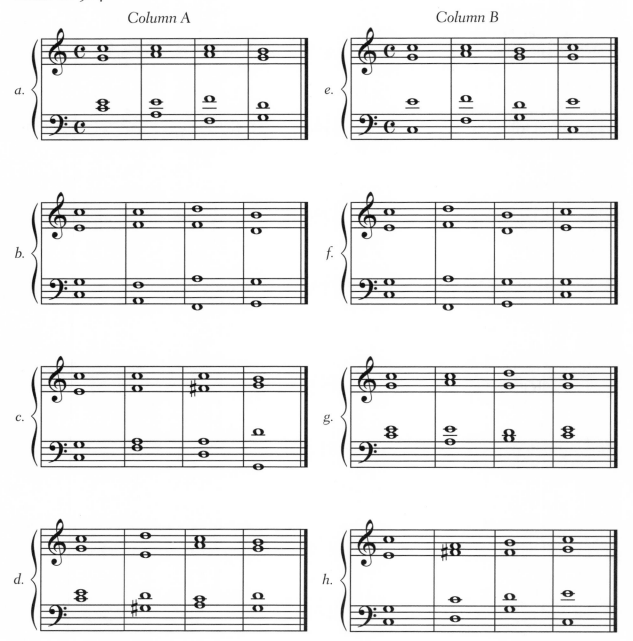

EXAMPLE 5.15

Column A   Column B

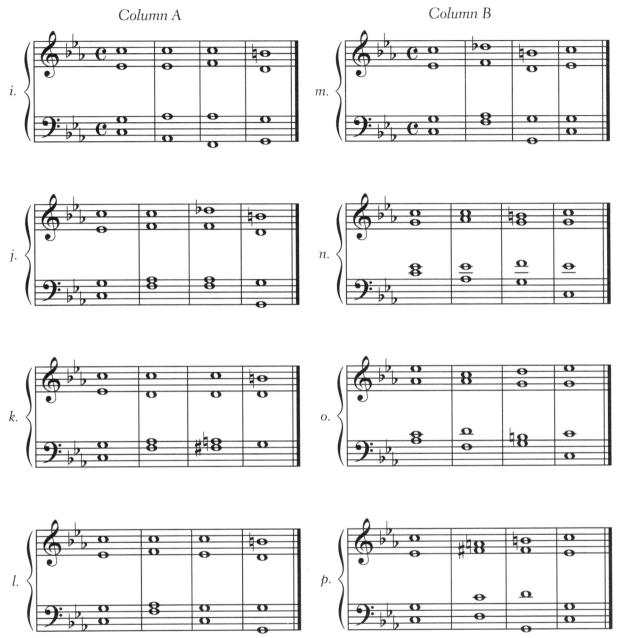

2. As in the previous game, decide on an order for your patterns. Assign the melody for each pattern to a different player, and choose a key and a meter for your improvisation.

3. Play through the set of progressions with all players using ostinati.

4. Play it through again, adding the melodies. The difference between this game and the previous one is that in this version the melodies must be motivically related. The first player is free to play whatever he or she likes. The second player must listen carefully to the first, and copy at least one element or motive in his or her melody, and so on.

5. When you are fluent in this style, replace the ostinati with real bass line and accompaniment patterns. The bass line should always be played by the lowest instrument except when it is that player's turn for the melody, in which case the bass line should be played by the instrument next lowest in range. This means that at any given time there will be one melody player, one bass line player, and two harmony players.

Swing Your Partner Round and Round (a game for 4 or more players)

The title for this game comes from square dancing, in which one of the musicians, known as the "caller," announces the moves the dancers are to follow. In this game, you will each have a turn to be "caller" of a chord progression.

1. Decide on a key and a meter for your improvisation. Choose one person to start as caller.

2. The caller should think of a short harmonic progression. Start with only four bars at first. You might want to set up some ground rules, such as "all progressions must begin with a I chord" or "all progressions must end on a V chord." Use only one harmony per bar to start.

3. Announce the chosen progression. If you have a blackboard available, you may write the Roman numerals on it, but do not write out the pitches.

4. Play the progression as a group using only long notes; don't worry about creating a melody or any rhythmic patterns. The first goal is to see if the ensemble can correctly realize the given chords. Whoever calls the progression should play the root of every chord. This will give the others something to build on and will ensure that the foundation of the chord sequence is correct. When you are comfortable, add some chords in inversions.

Here are some sample progressions. All chords except the Neapolitan chord in the last progression are to be played in root position:

I–IV–V–I
I–ii–V–I
I–vi–V–I
i–iv–V–i
i–N^6–V–i

Note that these all follow the same formula: tonic, some predominant, dominant, tonic. The challenge with these progressions is to figure out which notes each person needs to play to create the predominant called for.

Here are some progressions that follow a different pattern. What is the common link here?

I–vi–V/V–V
I–V/IV–IV–I
I–V–V/vi–vi

After you have played through the plain progression a few times, add melody and inner-voice patterns. Once your group is fluent in four-bar progressions, try a longer progression, about eight bars or so.

When you start creating longer phrases, you need to pay more attention to phrase structure and harmonic rhythm. Here is one way to create a simple phrase: choose both ends and then fill in the middle.

Let's say you want your phrase to begin and end on I. That takes care of two of your eight bars:

I———————I

Your final I chord will probably be the resolution of some sort of cadence. For this example, we'll use an authentic cadence, so we can put a V chord in the next-to-last bar:

I——————V–I

Now, what to do with those five empty bars? We could simply string together two of the smaller four-bar phrases you have already used, as follows:

I–IV–V–I–I–ii–V–I

There is nothing wrong with this grouping of chords. It would be more interesting, however, if we made some slight changes. Right now our eight-bar phrase is easily divisible into two four-bar phrases. Let's see if we can spread out the musical tension so that we really have one eight-bar phrase. The problem is what's happening in bars 3–5. The V–I cadence in bars 3 and 4 creates the feeling that this is the end of the phrase, and the repeated I chord just feels static. But if we avoided resolving that V chord and substituted something else for the I chord, we could spread out the tension and keep the phrase going. Here's one way we could alter our phrase:

I–IV–V–V/vi–vi–ii–V–I

This has a much different feel from the previous example, with only two chord changes. Changing our two I chords in bars 4 and 5 to V/vi and vi, respectively, keeps the direction of the music going and tells the listener that the phrase is not over.

Just as there are strong and weak beats within a bar, there are also strong and weak moments within a phrase. These moments are usually determined by the placement of various harmonies. One of the main elements that shapes the phrase is the length of time that each harmony lasts. As you saw before, this is called the "harmonic rhythm." The importance of harmonic rhythm in giving direction to a phrase is more obvious in phrases that contain more than one harmony per bar. In our example, and in most of the exercises in this book, the harmonic rhythm is very regular. As you gain experience, you can use a more irregular harmonic rhythm, with some chords being held over more than one bar and others changing more rapidly within the space of a measure. This will make your progressions much more interesting.

Another factor that shapes the phrase is the relationship between tension and resolution. Chords that are dissonant or that produce a feeling of tension, like dominant or diminished seventh chords, draw attention to themselves. The stress in these chords creates a strong moment in the phrase. When the dissonant chords arrive at consonant resolutions, weaker or more relaxing moments occur. Of course, sometimes a dissonant chord does not resolve in the expected way. In this case, the surprise of the "resolution" may create more tension, not less. And sometimes the harmonic rhythm thwarts this effect, particularly if dominant harmonies occur at the end of one bar and lead into a strong resolution at the beginning of the next bar. As you can see, the shape of a phrase is influenced by many factors. This is why the same basic sonorities can produce phrases of endless variety.

This is another great game to use as an encore at concerts or as an exercise in studio classes. Audience members could call out Roman numerals or pick phrase fragments out of a hat, and then watch with amazement as you string them all together.

Appendix A: Music Theory Review

The following pages provide a review of the theory and harmonic practice on which the preceding games are based. Each kind of chord you may encounter in the exercises is described here, along with some basic information on scales, sequences, and other compositional devices. This appendix is by no means a substitution for a music theory textbook! There are many more intricacies to music theory than are described here, but this should provide you with a starting point for understanding how some of the building blocks of music are constructed.

Pitches and Clefs

Most of the exercises in this book are written in treble and bass clefs. The string quartet examples also feature alto clef, used for the viola line. Clefs which look like the alto clef are called "C clefs" because the line that runs through the center of the clef represents middle C. Tenor clef, often used for the high register of the cello, looks like the alto clef but is placed one line higher on the staff; again, that line which runs through the center of the clef represents middle C.

Pitches in treble, or G, clef:

EXAMPLE A1

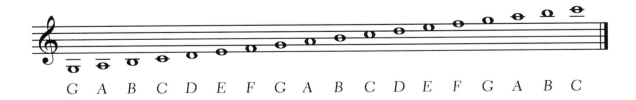

G A B C D E F G A B C D E F G A B C

EXAMPLE A2   Pitches in alto, or C, clef:

C D E F G A B C D E F G A B C D E F

EXAMPLE A3   Pitches in bass, or F, clef:

C D E F G A B C D E F G A B C D E F

Scales

The two most frequently found examples of scales in Western music are major and minor. Both of these scales are made up of whole steps and half steps; the only difference between the two kinds is the location of the half steps.

Major scales are constructed using half steps between scale degrees 3 and 4 and between 7 and 8. All the other intervals in the scale are whole steps. No matter what pitch we start on, if we build our scale with half steps in these places, we will create a major scale. The C major scale is the only one which can be created without accidentals; all other scales require the chromatic alteration of one or more notes in order to satisfy the whole step/half step layout.

C major scale (V-shaped brackets indicate half steps):

EXAMPLE A4

A major scale (accidentals mark notes that have been chromatically altered):

EXAMPLE A5

Minor scales come in three basic flavors: natural, harmonic, and melodic. Again, it is the different arrangement of whole and half steps that gives each variant of the minor scale its characteristic sound. All minor scales have a half step between scale degrees 2 and 3, but the location of the other half step(s) in the scale may vary.

The natural minor scale has half steps between scale degrees 2 and

3 and between 5 and 6. The a natural minor scale is shown below. Like C major, the a natural minor scale requires no accidentals. All other scales (and all other variants of the a minor scale) will need accidentals.

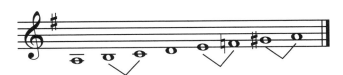

The natural minor definitely has a different color than the major scale, but it lacks the strong energy of the raised 7th degree pulling toward the tonic a half step above. In order to reclaim this powerful melodic and harmonic feature, a third half step was added to the natural minor to create the harmonic minor scale, which has half steps between scale degrees 2 and 3, 5 and 6, *and* 7 and 8. The raising of the 7th degree also results in the creation of an augmented second between scale degrees 6 and 7, which gives the scale its signature sound.

Harmonic minor scale:

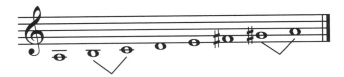

While the harmonic minor scale does have the advantage of the sense of direction created by the raised leading tone, the augmented second it also contains is an unwieldy interval that is too heavily spiced for regular use in most Western music. A third kind of minor scale, the melodic minor scale, represents the best of both worlds and offers many options to the composer or improvising musician. The melodic minor scale is the only one in which the ascending scale is different from the descending scale. It borrows the raised 6th and 7th degrees from the major scale on the ascending half, and copies the natural minor scale on the descending half.

The ascending melodic minor scale has half steps between scale degrees 2 and 3 and 7 and 8 only. It appears below:

By borrowing both scale degrees 6 and 7 from the major scale, composers can approach the tonic degree from below with a strong sense of melodic direction, but without the overwhelming flavor of the augmented second found in the harmonic minor scale. The half step between scale degrees 2 and 3 is maintained, however, as this is one of the fundamental signifiers of a minor modality.

The descending version of the melodic minor scale is the same as the natural minor:

EXAMPLE A9

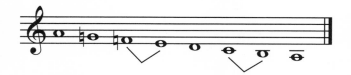

In common practice, what this plethora of minor-mode options means is that you have quite a lot of flexibility when making melodies using the upper half of the minor scale. The 3rd degree of the scale must always remain lowered (else the scale will no longer sound minor), but you can experiment freely to find whether the raised or lowered 6th or 7th degrees best suit your purposes.

In addition to major and minor, you can also use chromatic, whole-tone, or octatonic scales. Chromatic scales are simply those in which all the intervals are half steps. They may be spelled using sharps or flats depending on the key and direction. Because all of the intervals are half steps, it is hard to use this scale to communicate tonality: everything

EXAMPLE A10 sounds like "ti–do."

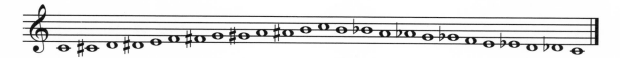

Just as the chromatic scale is all half steps, the whole-tone scale is all whole steps. It too may be spelled with either sharps or flats. Since there are no half steps in this scale to help pull toward a tonal center, the whole-tone scale is also not very functional in tonal harmony. Most of the time, whole-tone music either is atonal or follows some other system of tonal organization. If you look at the piano keyboard, you will see that there are only two possible whole-tone scales: the one beginning on C and the one beginning on C♯. Any other starting pitch will produce a scale that falls enharmonically into one or the other of these two categories.

EXAMPLE A11 Whole-tone scale beginning on C:

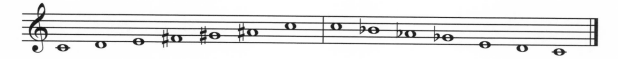

EXAMPLE A12 Whole-tone scale beginning on C♯/D♭:

You may also want to experiment with octatonic scales, which involve an alternating pattern of half and whole steps. You may begin with either a half step or a whole step, but after that you must alternate one half step with one whole step, as follows:

EXAMPLE A13

Like whole-tone scales, octatonic scales do not promote a strong sense of tonality, but they can frequently be found in loosely tonal pieces from the early twentieth century onward, and they are often used in jazz.

Intervals

An interval is the distance from one pitch to another. You have already seen the use of intervals (half steps and whole steps, also called minor and major seconds, respectively) to build scales, but intervals are also the building blocks of chords.

There are two parts to the description of an interval: type and quality. "Type" refers to the size of the interval: unison, second, third, fourth, fifth, sixth, seventh, or octave (or, sometimes, intervals beyond the octave). "Quality" tells us whether the interval is major, minor, augmented, diminished, or perfect. A given interval may be a "major sixth" or a "minor third" or an "augmented fourth," etc.

Determining the type of a given interval is easy, since it only involves counting letter names (scale degrees or lines and spaces could also be used). Identify the lower pitch of the interval by name. Counting that as "1," count upward until you reach the pitch name of the higher pitch. This tells you the type of interval. For example, from E up to B is a fifth. From E up to F is only a second. From E up to C is a sixth.

Determining the quality of an interval is a little harder. There are many different ways to approach this problem; my students usually do well by using the major scale as a "ruler" to help figure out an interval's quality. For right now, we will only be concerned with the quality of seconds, thirds, sixths, and sevenths. If the pitches in the interval are the same as the ones found in the major scale starting on the lower pitch of the interval, then the interval is major. Take the following example:

EXAMPLE A14

By counting the pitch names between E and C♯, we find that this is some kind of sixth. We now have to determine its quality. The first step is to build a major scale starting on the lower note of the interval:

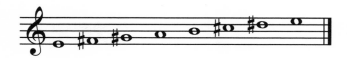

We see that C♯ is the version of the note C which occurs naturally in the E major scale. Therefore, this is a major sixth. Similarly, the following intervals are also major. Can you identify them?

EXAMPLE A16

Minor intervals are one half step smaller than major intervals. You might think that if the major scale can tell us about major intervals, then the minor scale should be able to tell us about minor intervals. Unfortunately, because of many factors including the mutability of the minor scale, it's not a good ruler. But as long as we have the major scale as our benchmark, we can figure out all other intervals by comparing them to the intervals in the major scale.

Here is another example:

EXAMPLE A17

We can find the type of the interval by counting up letter names, just as we did with the major interval. By counting up from B to A (we don't need to worry about accidentals when figuring out the type of interval that we have), we see that this is some kind of seventh. Now we need to determine its quality. Just as we did in the last example, we first begin by building a major scale on the lower pitch of the interval.

EXAMPLE A18

This time, though, we don't find our upper note in the scale. Therefore, it is not a major interval and must have some other quality. In order to figure out what quality it has, we can compare it to the major interval and see whether it is larger or smaller, and by how much. Here is a comparison of the major interval to our interval:

EXAMPLE A19

M7

As you can see, the top note in our interval is one half step lower than it would be in the major scale version. This means the interval is minor.

If you compare the major and minor scales (any variant), you will see that scale degrees 1, 4, 5, and 8 remain unchanged no matter where the half steps fall in the scale. Unisons, fourths, fifths, and octaves are not considered to be either major or minor; instead, they are called "perfect" regardless of whether they appear in a major key or a minor one.

Major and perfect intervals can also be augmented (made a half step larger), and minor and perfect intervals may be diminished (made a half step smaller). Again, use the major scale as your benchmark and calculate all alterations from the major interval.

EXAMPLE A20

dim6   m6   M6   aug6   dim5   P5   aug5

Intervals may also be inverted (flipped upside down so that the top note becomes the bottom note). The sum of the numbers that represent the type of a pair of inverted intervals will always be nine: a second inverted becomes a seventh (and vice versa), a third inverted becomes a sixth, a fourth becomes a fifth, and an octave becomes a unison.

When inverted, major intervals become minor (and vice versa), and diminished intervals become augmented (and vice versa). Perfect intervals remain perfect.

What would the inversions be of each of the following intervals?

· major third
· diminished seventh
· perfect fifth
· minor second
· augmented fourth

Chords

The fundamental interval used to build chords is the third. Other intervals may occur in chords, but they are most often a result of the chord being inverted so that different pitches are on the top or bottom. There are certain kinds of chords in which pitches that aren't part of this chain of thirds may occur (augmented sixth chords, chords with added sixths, etc.), but most of the exercises in this book use chords that are constructed simply by stacking major and minor thirds on top of each other.

EXAMPLE A21

The pitch used as the foundation of the stack of thirds is the root. All other chord tones are calculated from this pitch. Later on, when we review inversions of chords, we will learn that the root is not always the lowest-sounding note! But for now, we will build all of our chords with the root in the bass.

A major triad is constructed by placing a major third above the root, and a minor third above that. A minor triad also contains one major third and one minor third, but the order is reversed: the minor third is on the bottom and the major third is on the top. The first note above the root is called the third, and the one on top is called the fifth. These refer to their distance from the root.

EXAMPLE A22

Major   Minor

A chord made up of two minor thirds is a diminished chord. The distance from the root to the fifth is a diminished fifth. Similarly, a chord made up of two major thirds is an augmented triad; the distance from the root to the fifth is an augmented fifth.

EXAMPLE A23

Diminished   Augmented

When we do Roman numeral analysis of a harmonic progression, we are trying to figure out not just whether a chord is major or minor, but what place it occupies within the key. Is it the chord built on scale degree 1, the "home" chord that we call the tonic? Is it the chord built on scale degree 5, which we call the dominant? A C major chord may feel like home in one phrase, but in another it may sound as if it's going somewhere else. Using a Roman numeral system rather than just calling it "a C major chord" helps us identify how the chord functions within the context of the phrase. For that reason, this approach to harmonic analysis is called "functional harmony."

In order to figure out these Roman numerals, we will build a series of chords on the notes of the major scale. If we restrict ourselves to using only the notes of that scale in building our chords (in other words, no chromatic alterations), then we'll come up with a collection of both major and minor chords.

We number each degree of the scale with a Roman numeral. We use an uppercase or capital Roman numeral if the chord built on that scale degree is a major chord, and a lower-case Roman numeral if the chord is minor.

CM: I   ii   iii   IV   V   vi   vii°   I

You will see that the chord built on scale degree 7 is neither major nor minor, but diminished. This is indicated in the notation by a small circle placed at the top right edge of the Roman numeral. Because diminished chords are more closely related to minor chords than anything else, they take an altered form of the minor (lowercase) Roman numeral.

In major keys, the chords built on scale degrees I, IV, and V are always major, and the chords built on scale degrees ii, iii, and vi are always minor. The chord built on vii is always diminished.

In minor keys things get a bit more complicated because of the various versions of the minor scale and the desire to have the option of a raised 7th degree that gives a sense of pull toward the tonic. This tricky 7th scale degree appears naturally in three different chords of the minor scale: those built on scale degrees 3, 5, and 7. Because we use the chords built on scale degrees 5 and 7 to give a sense of harmonic pull toward the tonic, we generally use the raised form of scale degree 7 borrowed from the major or harmonic minor scale in building those chords. The chord built on scale degree 3, which has scale degree 7 as its fifth, uses the flattened version of scale degree 7 found in the natural minor scale, since it does not have any particular pull toward the tonic for which the raised seventh degree would be necessary. You will find exceptions to this rule, but this is a safe assumption for most of the music you'll encounter on a daily basis.

cm: i   ii°   III   iv   V   VI   vii°   i

As you can see from the example, in minor keys, i and iv are minor, III and VI are major, and ii and vii are diminished. (When the vii chord is built on the lowered 7th degree of the scale rather than on the raised leading tone, it becomes a major chord and functions as a secondary dominant; we'll review those in a moment.) The chord built on scale degree 5 is tricky, since it also includes that ambiguous 7th scale degree. Spelling it diatonically in a minor key yields a minor triad which does not have the same pull toward the tonic as its major counterpart. This is because the third of the minor v chord is the lowered 7th degree of the scale, not the raised leading tone that naturally occurs when constructing V in a major key. In order to get that sense of the chord pulling toward resolution to the tonic, we habitually borrow the raised 7th scale degree from the melodic (or harmonic) version of the minor scale and substitute that for the lowered version that occurs naturally in the key. Thus, the chord built on scale degree 5 would naturally come out minor, but in most circumstances we borrow an accidental to make it major and give it the same dominant function it would have in a major key.

Each scale degree has a particular name that indicates its function:

I: tonic
ii: supertonic
iii: mediant
IV: subdominant
V: dominant
VI: submediant
vii: leading tone (or "subtonic," if not built on the raised 7th degree)

Inversions

Just like intervals, chords may also be inverted. This means that the root of the chord is not necessarily the lowest-sounding pitch. The advantage to inverting chords is that it makes our bass lines more interesting.

When a chord has been inverted, we attach certain Arabic numerals to the Roman numeral. (A Roman numeral without any attached Arabic numerals is understood to be in root position, in which the root is in the bass.) These Arabic numerals, which come from the figured-bass tradition, indicate the presence of other tones in the chords at specified intervals up from the bass note (not the root!). Since we understand that chords are generally made up of thirds, it's not necessary to indicate that there are other thirds in the chord; we only need to use Arabic figures to show the presence of other kinds of intervals up from the bass. Look at the following examples:

I^6—this indicates a major I chord, inverted so that there exists a sixth above the bass note. (All other intervals are assumed to be thirds, so it's not necessary to specify that with a number.) This is a chord in its first inversion, in which the third of the triad is in the bass. Whenever you see a Roman numeral marked only with an Arabic 6, it's a first-inversion chord.

IV$^6_4$—this indicates a major IV chord, arranged in such a way that there exists in the chord a sixth above the bass and a fourth above the bass. This chord is in its second inversion, in which the fifth of the triad is in the bass. Chords marked with $^6_4$ are always second-inversion chords. See the examples below:

Key of C:

EXAMPLE A26

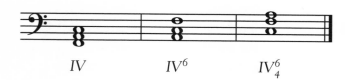

IV   IV^6 IV$^6_4$

Sometimes, when students encounter a written-out chord in an inversion, they have a hard time recognizing what the root of the chord is (which also determines what Roman numeral the chord should receive). A good solution for this is to use the alphabet method:

1. Write out the alphabet from A to G twice in a row.
2. Identify the bass of the chord. Circle that letter name in your alphabet row.
3. Identify another chord tone. Look for that letter in your alphabet row. You're looking for it to be a third away from something you have already circled.
4. When you have finished identifying all the pitches in the chord, you should have a row of circles that are a third apart from one another. The leftmost circled pitch is the root of the chord.

As an example, let's use this as our mystery chord:

GM: ?

First, I write out the alphabet. I write it out twice because I want to be sure that I'll have all my circled notes in a row so it's easy to read.

A B C D E F G A B C D E F G

I find my bass note and circle it.

A B C D E F G Ⓐ B C D E F G

Then I find the other pitches and circle them, looking for a complete set of chord tone letters that are each a third away from other chord tones (in other words, only one letter is skipped between circled notes).

A B C Ⓓ E Ⓕ G Ⓐ B C D E F G

Once I have all the chord tones circled, with no more than one letter skipped between circled notes, then I know that the root of the chord is the circled pitch name furthest to the left, which in this case is D.

Now I must figure out what Roman and Arabic numerals to assign this chord. I need to use the root of the chord, not the bass, to figure out what the Roman numeral is. My root is D. In the key of G, D is scale degree 5. So this is some kind of V chord. I usually expect the V chord to be major, but I should double check to make sure there's no chromatic alteration that would change that. Yes, we have D, F♯, and A, so it is indeed major. So I'll need a capital Roman numeral V. In order to figure out the Arabic numerals I need, I have to know what degree of the chord is in the bass. The bass is A, which is the fifth of the chord. When the fifth of the chord is in the bass, the chord is in its second inversion and takes the numerals 6 and 4. Therefore, we would identify this chord as follows:

GM: IV$^6_4$

Seventh Chords

If we take a regular old triad and stack yet another third on top of it, we've created a seventh chord. It's called a seventh chord because the distance from the root to the extra added note is some kind of seventh. Just as we saw when creating simple triads, it's the quality (major or minor) of the newly added third that changes the sonority of the seventh chord.

There are five kinds of seventh chords that you are likely to run into in Western music. Let's begin with seventh chords that are built using major triads as the foundation.

The most common kind of seventh chord is called the dominant seventh chord. It's called this because it's most frequently built on the dominant (5th) scale degree. It creates such a strong sense of pulling toward a tonic triad that if you build this chord on any other degree of the scale you will create the impression of modulation. The dominant seventh chord is made of a major triad with a minor third added to the top. For this reason, it's also called a major-minor seventh chord (abbreviated Mm7).

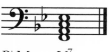

B♭M: V^7

We add an Arabic numeral 7 to the Roman numeral to show that a seventh above the root has been added. We will examine the inversions of these seventh chords in just a moment.

Another kind of seventh chord may be formed by taking a major triad and adding a major third to the top. This is called a major-major seventh chord, or sometimes just a major seventh chord (abbreviated MM7 or M7).

B♭M: IV^7

Unlike the dominant seventh, MM7 chords are not generally built on the dominant. They are used primarily to add color to existing chords, not to give an increased sense of direction to the phrase. They are also popular in jazz.

There is only one kind of common seventh chord that takes a minor triad as its foundation. This is called the minor-minor seventh chord (or sometimes just a minor seventh chord, abbreviated mm7 or m7), and it's built by adding a minor third to a minor triad.

EXAMPLE A30

B♭M: iv⁷

These are often built on ii, vi, or iii chords.

The two remaining common seventh chords both use the diminished triad as a foundation. The first, made by combining a diminished triad with a major third, is called the half-diminished seventh chord (abbreviated $^{ø}_{7}$). It's often found built on scale degree ii in a minor key.

EXAMPLE A31

gm: ii$^{ø}_{7}$

The last kind of seventh chord is the fully-diminished seventh chord (sometimes just called a diminished seventh chord), and it is formed by taking a diminished triad and adding another minor third on top. Abbreviated as $^{o}_{7}$, it is most commonly found built on the raised scale degree 7 in either major or minor keys.

EXAMPLE A32

gm: vii$^{o}_{7}$

Inversions of Seventh Chords

Because the intervals formed when seventh chords are inverted are different from those formed with the inversion of simple triads, the Arabic numerals that indicate inversions of seventh chords are different from those that indicate inversions of triads. Also, because seventh chords contain four different pitches that could appear in the bass, there is one more possible inversion for seventh chords than there is for simple triads. The good news, though, is that the Arabic numerals do not change based on the quality of the seventh chord.

The first inversion, in which the third of the chord is in the bass, gets the numerals $^{6}_{5}$.

The second inversion, in which the fifth is in the bass, gets the numerals $^{4}_{3}$.

The third inversion, in which the seventh is in the bass, gets the numerals $^{4}_{2}$.

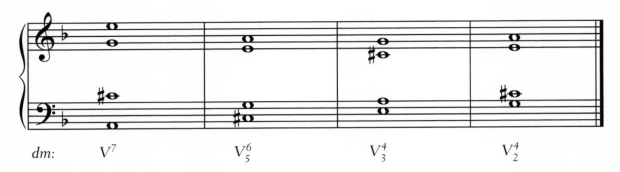

dm: V⁷   V⁶₅   V⁴₃   V⁴₂

You'll notice that the Arabic numerals don't say anything about the voicing of the other pitches in the chord; they only specify which chord tone is in the bass. Also, note that this example is in a minor key, so the 7th scale degree (C) had to be chromatically raised (to C♯) in order to make the foundational triad of the V chord major. Whenever you are working in a minor key, you will need to raise the leading tone by manually adding the appropriate accidental if you want that V chord to function as a dominant. The key signature does not take care of that for you the way it does in a major key.

Secondary Dominants

When we first reviewed the dominant seventh chord, you read that if you built that chord on any other degree of the scale, you'd be on your way to modulating to a new key. Many modulations happen exactly that way, including some of the ones in this book. This is called creating a "secondary dominant"—a chord that functions as a dominant of some other key than the original (a secondary key), and that propels the harmonic motion toward a cadence in that new key. You can achieve this effect with either a regular major triad or with a dominant seventh chord.

Remember that in functional harmony, chords are identified by Roman numerals based on how they function, not on what pitch names they include. Because a secondary dominant functions in relation to a different key, we change its notation to reflect that. Depending on which theory book you read, you will find different ways of notating that relationship; in this book, we use the following notation: V⁷/IV.

This means that the chord functions as a dominant seventh chord that wants to resolve to the key of scale degree 4. In other words, if we were in the key of scale degree 4, that chord would be a V⁷ chord.

When in doubt as to whether a chord is a secondary dominant, let your ears be your guide. Does the chord want to resolve to the original key, or to a new one? Secondary dominants will also almost always include some form of chromatic alteration, so that's another clue that a shift in tonality might be on the way.

The following progression contains a secondary dominant, notated below the staff:

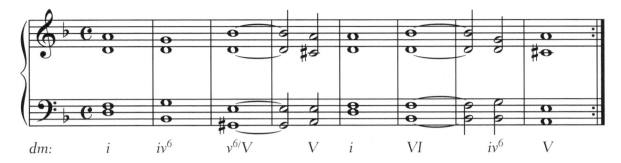

dm: i   iv⁶   v⁶/V   V   i   VI   iv⁶   V

Neapolitan and Augmented Sixth Chords

These are two highly colorful kinds of chords that can add a lot of life to your improvisations. Although augmented sixth chords can sometimes be found in major keys, both they and Neapolitan chords tend to appear much more frequently in minor keys.

The Neapolitan chord is a major chord built on the flattened 2nd degree of the minor scale. Because it almost always is used in its first inversion, it's often referred to as a "Neapolitan sixth" chord (the "sixth" refers to the Arabic numeral that marks the inversion). It's generally notated below the staff as N⁶. It functions as a predominant (something that leads to the V chord), generally in place of the ii°, iv, or VI chord.

dm:

The following example uses a Neapolitan sixth chord:

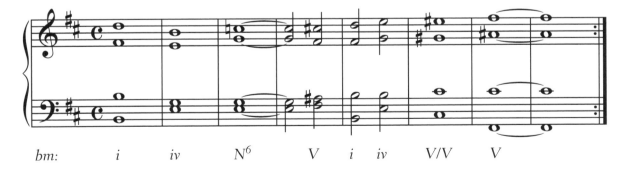

bm: i   iv   N⁶   V   i   iv   V/V   V

The augmented sixth chords also function as predominants, although they are a little trickier to construct. As we found in our review of the harmonic minor scale, half steps are very important in creating a sense of direction. In order to heighten a sense of progression toward the V chord, the opposite in polarity of the I chord, the augmented sixth chord approaches scale degree 5 via a half step—in both directions. It includes both the pitch that is a half step below scale degree 5 and the pitch that's a half step above it.

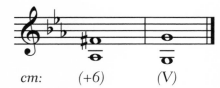

cm: (+6)   (V)

The easiest way to build these chords is to refer to the scale degrees we need to include. Augmented sixth chords come in four national flavors: Italian, German, French, and Swiss. We'll begin with the Italian, as it is the simplest. The pitches needed for an Italian augmented sixth chord are ♭6, 1, and ♯4.

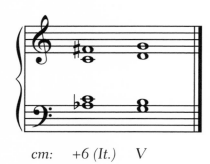

cm: +6 (It.)   V

All of the other national variants include the same three notes as the Italian, but with one additional note that varies the flavor somewhat. The French sixth chord takes the Italian ♭6, 1, and ♯4 and adds scale degree 2 to it:

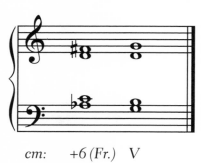

cm: +6 (Fr.)   V

The German uses ♭6, 1, ♯4, and ♭3:

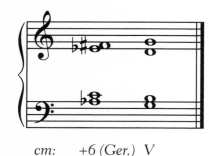

cm: +6 (Ger.)   V

And the Swiss uses ♭6, 1, ♯4, and ♯2:

cm: +6 *(Sw.)* I_4^6

In sonority, the Swiss augmented sixth is enharmonically equivalent to the German, although it is spelled differently. Notice that the Swiss sixth in this example resolves to I_4^6, which is very common with augmented sixth progressions. Were the progression to continue, the I_4^6 would almost certainly be followed by a V chord before arriving at the final tonic chord.

Augmented sixth chords are difficult to describe using Roman and Arabic numerals. It is possible to do so, but the resultant descriptions tend to be wordy and awkward. For this reason, we tend to notate them simply as "+6" below the staff, with the national marker in parentheses.

An augmented sixth chord appears in the following progression and is notated appropriately below the staff:

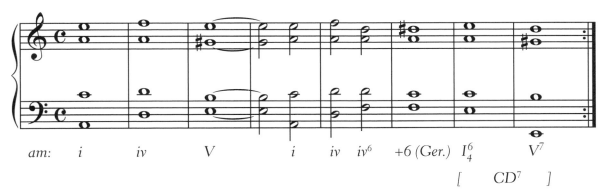

am: *i*   *iv*   *V*   *i*   *iv* iv^6 +6 *(Ger.)* I_4^6 V^7

[CD^7]

As in the Swiss sixth example above, the augmented sixth in this progression resolves to a I_4^6, which is here followed by a V chord. This progression of I_4^6–V is one of the most commonly used progressions in Western music. It has also caused tons of pedagogical conflict, because scholars do not agree on the best way to describe this progression. Most argue that in the second inversion, and followed by a V chord, the I_4^6 chord doesn't really function like a tonic chord, which normally gives us a sense of finality and completion. Instead, they hear the notes of the I chord as an ornamentation of the V chord, and argue that the whole thing functions as a big dominant chord. Others are uncomfortable with assigning it a Roman numeral V, since the first half of the progression clearly involves the notes of the I chord. One of the many solutions, and the one used in this book, is to call this progression a cadential dominant, abbreviated CD (or CD^7 if the V chord contains a seventh). When the term CD or "cadential dominant" is used in this book, it's understood to mean a I_4^6–V progression.

Non-Harmonic Tones

If a piece were composed only of chord tones, it would be very consonant, but probably not very interesting. Non-harmonic tones (pitches that don't fit neatly into the chord structure) are necessary to give our improvisations and compositions more interest and style. Non-harmonic tones come in several varieties. The kinds we will review here are passing tones, neighbor tones, and appoggiaturas. All of these non-harmonic tones can be either diatonic (using only notes found in the key) or chromatic (artificially raised or lowered via accidentals).

Passing tones occur when a skip between two melodic notes is filled in with all of the non-chord tones that occur on the intervening steps between those two notes. Passing tones must always occur by step, and they must "pass" from one note to the other; in other words, you are not allowed to skip any steps in the line.

EXAMPLE A43

Passing tones are very useful to us when constructing improvisations based on a chord progression, because they allow us to connect notes from one chord to another in a melodically interesting way. For example, when making a melody, you may want to get from the alto voice of one chord to the tenor voice of another. Using passing tones can smooth the transition and allow you to connect the chords in a musically satisfying way.

Another kind of non-harmonic tone is the neighbor tone. Like the passing tone, the neighbor tone proceeds by step away from the originating chord tone, but instead of proceeding on to another chord tone, the neighbor tone turns around and goes back to the originating tone.

EXAMPLE A44

The terms *passing* and *neighbor tones* are used only to refer to non-harmonic tones in stepwise motion that occur on the weak part of the beat or bar. A non-harmonic tone that falls on the strong portion of the beat or bar may be an accented passing tone (which follows the same rules as a regular passing tone) or a special kind of non-harmonic tone called an appoggiatura. The name is taken from the Italian verb *appoggiare*, meaning "to lean." Like passing and neighbor tones, appoggiature resolve in stepwise motion and may be either diatonic or chromatic. The resolution of an appoggiatura always occurs on the weak part of the beat or bar.

EXAMPLE A45

In the first bar, the appoggiatura is in the soprano; in the second bar, it occurs in the alto. As you see from the third bar, appoggiature (and other non-harmonic tones) may sometimes appear in two voices simultaneously. What you see in bar three is called a double appoggiatura.

There are plenty of other kinds of non-harmonic tones that can add a lot of flavor to your improvisations. You can find descriptions and examples of these in most music theory textbooks.

Appendix B: Additional Harmonic Progressions

Here are some additional harmonic progressions you can use for improvisation. Many of these are more advanced than the ones attached to the preceding exercises. They may include secondary dominants, augmented sixth chords, Neapolitan chords, and other chromatic chords. Some of the progressions are realized for you; for others, only the Roman numeral notation is provided. Write the harmonic analysis below each excerpt.

As you set about realizing the ones that are not already written out, you will have to make decisions about phrasing and harmonic rhythm. Most of the exercises in this book use eight-bar phrases, but in other musical examples you will find a wide variety of phrase lengths. By changing the harmonic rhythm of these progressions, you can start to experiment with building phrases of varying lengths.

a.

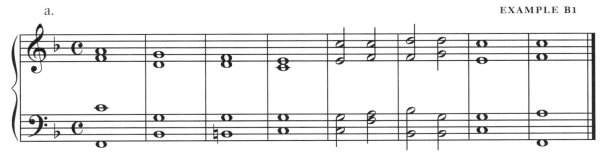

b.

c.

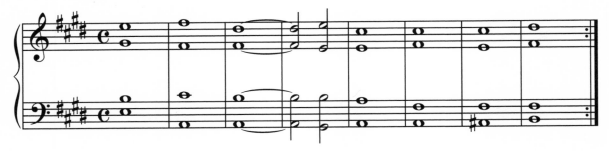

d.

e.

Progressions to Be Realized

MAJOR MODE

1. I–IV–V–vi–I–V–I
2. I–IV–V–vi–IV–ii$^{(7)}$–V–I
3. V–I–IV–vi–iii–IV–V–I
4. I^6–IV–V–vi–ii–CD*–I
5. I–IV^6–V^6–I–V–vi–IV–vii°–I–V
6. I–iii–IV–I–IV–CD–I
7. I–I^6–IV–V^7/vi–vi–V^7/V–V^7–I
8. vii°–I–I^6–IV–CD7–I
9. I–V^7/IV–IV–I–V^7/ii–V^7–I
10. I–V^4/V–V^6–I–I^6–IV–V–vi

* reminder: CD = cadential dominant, a I$^6_4$–V^7 progression.

1. $i–iv^6–V^6–i–VI–ii°–V^7–i$
2. $V^6–i–iv–ii°–CD–VI$
3. $ii°–V–VI–ii°–V–i–iv–i$
4. $i–VI–i–iv–V/V–V–\sharp vii°–i$
5. $i–V^6–i^6–V–VI–ii–V^7–i$
6. $i–i^6–ii°–V^6–VI^6–VI–IV–ii°–V^7–i$
7. $V^7–V^7/iv–iv–i–V^7/V–V^7–i$
8. $i–V^4–i–V^7/III–III–V^7/VI–VI–V^7–i$
9. $i–V/bVII–\flat VII–V/VI–VI–V/V–V^7–i$
10. $V^7–i–iv^7–V–III^7–VI–ii°–V–i–iv–V/V–V$

You should also try writing out some progressions of your own for your ensembles to play. Use the formulas presented here and earlier in the book as places to start, and see what happens if you experiment with substituting one chord for another, joining two phrases together, changing the tonality, changing the cadence type, etc.

NICOLE M. BROCKMANN enjoys a multifaceted career of teaching, performance, and scholarship. She holds a BFA in viola performance from Carnegie Mellon University and a DMA and other graduate degrees from Yale University. She is a past president of the Dalcroze [Eurhythmics] Society of America and has presented widely on topics involving Eurhythmics and musicianship. She has taught at Yale University and West Virginia University, and is currently on the faculty of the DePauw University School of Music, where she teaches viola, chamber music, and musicianship.